the
NEWNESS ADVANTAGE

—

GRAHAM COOKE

BOOK TWO
Letters from God Series
WWW.BRILLIANTBOOKHOUSE.COM

BRILLIANT BOOK HOUSE

PO Box 871450
Vancouver, WA 98687

ISBN: 978-0-9896262-6-2

All Scripture quotations are taken from the New American Standard Bible (Copyright © 1960, 1962, 1963, 1971, 1972, 1973, 1975, 1977, 1995 by The Lockman Foundation).

Please note that Brilliant Book House has made the stylistic choice to capitalize certain words and pronouns that refer to the Father, Son, and Holy Spirit, although it may differ from the stylistic choices of other publishers.

This book and all other materials published by Graham Cooke are available online at www.BrilliantBookHouse.com

If you would like more information on Graham Cooke and his ministry, please visit www.brilliantperspectives.com

Cover & Layout by Bethel Media

ACKNOWLEDGEMENTS

To the Brilliant Team who has been setting up in our new suite of offices on the fifth floor. It has been an interactive process to renovate the space, buy furniture and equipment, and to create a culture of relationship and creativity in the process. It's happening!

Together we are embarking on a creative journey that will upgrade the process of how we produce devotional, teaching, and training materials. We have been moving towards this for several years. The addition of a TV studio is a serious upgrade enabling us to move into a different level of spiritual communication.

Welcome to the 5th Wave.

A SPECIAL ACKNOWLEDGEMENT

I would also like to give special credit to Allison Bown who has been a personal friend and co-collaborator for many years.

Together we started and developed The Warrior Class an amazing company of prophetic intercessors who operate at the cutting edge of specific targeted prayer over events, cities and nations.

We have worked together on events and training programs for a number of years. Allison is a superb trainer and a great writer. Her books, *Joyful Intentionality and The Image,* have been very well received.

Allison is a brilliant processor of truth. She has an amazing grasp of the follow-through necessary to establish what the Holy Spirit has opened up for His people.

Allison is part of the creative writing team at Brilliant Perspectives and plays a key role in cultivating our training resources. She is an excellent speaker and trainer and is available for online consulta-tions for leadership teams and those looking to dive deeper into the resources that our Brilliant team offers.

To reach out to Allison Bown for development in these areas, please email *allisonbownoffice@gmail.com*

DEDICATION

Everything we are and do is because Jesus initiates our engagement and involvement. Without His sacrifice we are lost. The process of being found in Him is the key element of this book. Aided by the incomparable Holy Spirit, who brings all truth to stunning life within our hearts and circumstances, we are empowered to not only know Jesus as a living practical reality, but also to become like Him as we grow up in all things.

The gracious workmanship of the Father-Creator, the sublime Presence of Jesus within, and the always joyful Holy Spirit in our sanctification process is overwhelming and beautiful.

Together, the Three create, initiate, transform, and complete us!

CONTENTS

My unique perspective creates the lens of the Kingdom, which renews your thinking and elevates your identity in the new man. When you see yourself in and through the internal presence of Christ, you can relish Us in a greater way. All your life events and situations become the training ground for growth, renewal, refreshing, and identity.

Only a new identity in My Son can transform you to become like Him. The new covenant requires that you unlearn the old one. Likewise, the new man demands new perspective, mindset, and language. You will love the learning involved in the development of a habitational lifestyle because it will set you free from a visitational culture. All growth occurs when freedom partners with unlearning to create breakthrough.

There is one life: Christ in you, which provides the same privileges that He enjoys as a Son. There is the other side of that life: you are in Christ, which allows you to live in expectations that are greater than your circumstances. The security of My love empowers your weakness to become His fullness. You are experiencing a necessary and thrilling dependence that creates a newness of life. Growing up into all things in Christ opens up your inheritance in Him as you practice the lifestyle of being the beneficiaries of His will.

Grace is your introduction to glory. A lifestyle that is rich in grace shapes the way you see Me, others, and yourself. Grace elevates all relationships. Grace and righteousness combine to create a lasting freedom that allows a ruling power to emerge in you, guaranteeing Presence. Grace and truth create a newness advantage that is wonderfully vulnerable to My all-sufficiency. Grace empowers the process of becoming Christ-like.

Your identity in Jesus fills your life with love, peace, joy and the promise, favor, and faith of His internal Presence. Sanctification is the joyful process of reprogramming the will to come under the new man because you are being saved by His life. You are made alive together with Jesus. This is the key to enjoying transformation in Christ. As you pay attention to Our cheerfulness in you, the law of the Spirit of life in Christ overwhelms every negative.

All things were created through Christ and for Him, therefore He is your mirror image of Me and your place in My Presence. There is a wisdom and power in abiding in the Holy Spirit that overturns every negative aspect of life. The Spirit of Truth will always overcome every contradictory, pessimistic practice of the old nature. You are My habitation and as you relax into My Presence, Jesus' life rises up and makes all things new.

My intentions become the purposes of man. You respond to Jesus in every situation to receive the resources that He initiates. My nature towards you is the foundation of all your trust in Me. My unchanging heart and word become your deepest confidence regardless of circumstances. You are being trained in your life situations to receive My provisions that belong to the life of Christ in you.

I want you to think about how you see and perceive the world around you, how you think about what you're perceiving and how you talk about yourself, about Me and about others. With this in mind, how will you choose to behave?

INTRODUCTION

There are times when the world, life, events, and circumstances all seem to conspire against us. Our learned behavior in the world is constantly provoking us to see and act within a familiar system of logic, reason, transactional relationships, social norms, and nationalistic cultural expressions.

When we are learning also to become a new creation that is fixed on all things becoming new to the point where we are encouraged to set our minds on things above, not on things that are on Earth, we realize that we can be pulled in different directions. It is possible to become dualistic in our growth process.

Learning how to see, think, speak, and act like the new man in Jesus is the central part of all our life situations. It's the prime directive from God that requires our prime focus and interaction.

Engaging with Father, Son, and Holy Spirit in this life-changing transformation is the essence of this book. Written from the perspective of Their oneness and unity, we will discover God's intentional, delightful focus on us and His creative passion to overwhelm us with His loving, joyful, and peaceful Presence in all our circumstances as we grow up into all the fullness of Christ.

When we hear One, we hear them All. It is our joy to practice listening to Each and to learn to distinguish Their individual voices and build our relationship accordingly.

The newness advantage creates the foundation for a powerful perspective to emerge that shapes our thinking, language, and partnership with a God who Himself never changes, but who radically alters everyone with whom He connects.

Graham

PREPARING FOR A DIVINE CONVERSATION

You are about to engage with the passionate heart of God.

Take time to sit, read, and listen to what God desires to say to you and hear the resonant kindness, gentleness, and passion in His voice.

Pay attention to what rises up in your heart towards Him: gratitude, astonishment, relief, joy, affirmation, and possibly the desire to tell Him, "I *knew* life with You could be like this!" He loves to hear those words.

Embrace the challenges to your previous mindsets. Is this who you've known God to be—or is there a new experience of Him that emerges as you read?

Is there anything that surprises you? It's okay to be perplexed (Acts 10:17-20), but remember, God is not the author of confusion—you are. In your walk with the Lord He is always teaching you *how* to think because that is the definitive key to growth (Proverbs 23:7; Romans 12:2; 1 Corinthians 2:12-16). When He challenges your thinking, He creates an opportunity for you to *unlearn* something so that you are no longer stuck.

Think about the implications for God in the truth that He lays before you. If He gives you a command, a promise, or permission, then He has to act towards you in the same context as you, so that together you can explore the truth that sets you free.

For example, if He gives you permission to "Even so consider yourselves to be dead to sin, but alive to God in Christ Jesus" (Romans 6:11), this impacts Him and His relationship with you because He also must consider you dead, which means He cannot work on your old man or be sin-conscious towards you! He loves the implications and joyfully binds Himself to them for your sake!

Consider the questions of exploration that are embedded in these letters. They will help unwrap your thinking, expand your heart, and open up new possibilities.

When you receive a letter from a dear friend, you don't respond with an academic paper! Throughout these pages, there are invitations to craft personal letters back to God that capture your thoughts about His thoughts, your feelings about His passion and compassion for you.

You may keep precious letters from your loved ones and pore over them again and again. That's a great way to approach these letters from God. As you read and reread His letters to you, explore them more deeply each time. Notice *how* God's Presence is becoming more and more real to you.

When God presents you with truth, He is inviting you to upgrade your relationship with Him.

Here are some great questions to ask:

1. "What are the key truths here?"

2. "What aspects of God's nature are being revealed to me?"

3. "Who does He want to be for me in *this* situation?"

4. "What are the key breakthroughs in these truths?"

5. "What obstacle can I overcome with these truths?"

6. "What new part of my identity am I discovering in this dialogue?"

7. "What am I discovering that I would like to explore further?"

8. "What interaction with the Lord is available that I may not have considered before or am now considering in a fresh way?"

9. "If I lived in this upgrade, what would change for me?"

Take time out to write and reflect on it. Love the learning. If what you read clashes with your perception of truth, be a good Berean and search for the truth without prejudice (Acts 17:10-11).

There is no transformation outside of a renewed mind. Enjoy the journey into thinking differently and being with God in a fresh way.

LETTER 1

The Lens Through Which You View Life

KEY SCRIPTURES:
Exodus 6:30, 7:1; Acts 9-10; 1 Corinthians 2:12-16;
Ephesians 1:18, 4:2-24, 6:10; Colossians 3:1-3;
Philemon 6; Hebrews 8:13

Beloved,

As the Originator of all things, We have a unique perspective about everything We have created. Our rule of governance is from Heaven to Earth. It is a fixed and unchanging Kingdom outlook that allows people to rise above world events and personal dilemmas and experience the power of truth and faith combining to overcome any obstacle. This is the story of Scripture and Our unique place in the hearts of people.

Our perspective, truth, and faith offer an entirely different way of seeing, thinking, speaking, and acting. It is the way, the truth, and the life of how the Three of Us co-operate in the Kingdom. In making you in Our image, these are the areas of life that We are constantly seeking to address in Our people.

Beloved, the Earth must adjust to Heaven and its spiritual laws: the law of love, the law of liberty, the law of the Spirit of life in Christ Jesus, to name a few. It follows then that if your relationship with learning is from a world-based, logical, analytical, academic, systematic study, you may experience a disconnect with a Kingdom that works differently. In Heaven We pursue everything through relationship, trust, vision, imagination, creativity, faith, and the truth of Our unchanging nature.

Scripture constantly defines Our delight and willingness to step outside the bounds of man-made laws and conventions to express the wholeness of Heaven in the context of Earth. When you make Us in your image, you disconnect from Our lens and make yourself myopic in the process.

VISION THAT ELEVATES

When I wanted to send an emissary to the house of Cornelius, I chose Peter; a big-hearted, simple, trusting, passionate man who, most importantly for Me, was the only man to ask to step out of the boat when Jesus walked on water. Sure, he felt overwhelmed and sank—but that is *not* the story. The narrative that I was overjoyed to see was a man wanting and attempting to move in the way that is normal to Our lifestyle.

Of course when it came to asking a good Jewish man to go to a gentile house, which was against all the traditions of his faith and culture, I knew this was no small request. Yet I knew that Peter, in all his uncertainty and perplexity, would still do My bidding.

Peter grasping the meaning of the vision of the sheet that was lowered, which contained all kinds of non-kosher animals, combined with My invitation to kill and eat, was going to be challenging. I could not tell him everything up front. I simply cannot take the adventure element out of faith—that is where the joy resides!

The stress and strain of believing for something out of your reach must become the joy and peace in believing. The way to succeed in faith is to make Us greater than the issue.

Peter was not at that point when he left on his journey, but by the time he arrived at the house of Cornelius, he had opened his heart and was trusting Me in a new way. People change as they travel in faith, not by standing still waiting to understand everything. Peter would come to know that his own history, together with his lens change, would usher in a whole new era for the global gentile community. A new perspective in Peter began the process of elevating a people group, who only knew darkness, to enter the light of redemption.

A NEW LENS CREATES WHOLENESS

Saul, a powerful Pharisee who had completely missed both the coming and the purpose of My coming, was in a blind religious rage persecuting Kingdom people who seemed to him to be manifestly different from his own heritage.

All of his academic study, combined with a religious fervor, gave him a lens that said it was right to persecute and kill those who saw God in a different way. It was only when I showed up in brilliant light while he traveled to Damascus that he was able to come to his senses and start a different journey. Sitting in blindness for three days allowed him the opportunity to think differently and repent of his perspective.

What a wonderful journey We had with the one who would eventually embrace the gentile name Paul! How We enjoyed declaring the reality of the Kingdom and the truth of who We are, how We see things, and the way We like to work with Our people. Paul's lens change was radical and exciting. A judgmental, hate-filled man became the apostle of love and grace.

OUR PERSPECTIVE OF YOU CHANGES EVERYTHING

Moses desperately wanted Me to see and relate to him in the same way he saw himself. His expression of exclaimed surprise was funny: "See me as I really am! I cannot speak to Pharaoh." I knew exactly who Moses was without Me. He needed to understand who he could become *with* Me.

My response to his weakness was to tell him My strength in what I had called him to do: "See, I make you as God to Pharaoh, and your brother Aaron shall be your prophet." I was not inviting him to be the fourth member of the Trinity. I was telling him that with Me, he could walk at an unprecedented level above his opposition, obstacles, and circumstances.

Your perspective of yourself changes your thinking and creates a new language of agreement in faith. A new perspective, a new mindset, and a new language are the key elements of an upgraded identity. When I declare how I see you, I am asking you to look more closely at who you are becoming next.

It is not enough to know yourself in the context of your world experience. That will never be My frame of reference for you. My perspective gives you a context in the Kingdom, which must then override your earthly way of looking at yourself and your circumstances.

People with a natural mindset are always calling Me down into their weakness, rather than seeing that I am elevating them into My strength and power. Once Moses had settled into My way of seeing himself, we could partner in the destruction of all the household gods of Egypt and the liberation of Israel.

"Be strong in the Lord and in the strength of His might" is the only way that you can walk with Me and do the impossible. In our relationship I want you to get acquainted with Me, again understanding and enjoying all that I have done for you in Christ. As you learn to acknowledge the value, importance, and impact of the new man in Christ within you, then our fellowship together will have significant repercussions in the world.

YOUR LENS IS BEING CONSTANTLY RENEWED

As you are learning to walk with the new lens of the Kingdom, every circumstance provides opportunity to renew your way of perceiving. As you see differently, your mindset will form your new perspective. You will make constant necessary adjustments, turning away from your natural mind as you become more spiritually minded. This is the throne room of the mind of Christ in the new man. In Christ your new man receives the power to focus your mind on things above, not on things on Earth.

When your old man died, the new man replaced him. You are now perpetually hidden in Christ in Me. This means that I relate to you through My Son and you relate to Me from your position in Him. It's perfect! You bypass the world and go straight to Heaven in your lifestyle.

This works best as you get in the rhythm of putting off the old and embracing the new. Most people want new but think old. The natural mind can only change when it sees something different. First put off the old, then you are free to receive the mind of Christ.

It's give and take. Set your mind on desiring a higher way of thinking. As I begin to speak new things, you have a choice. In our relationship your new man partners with Me and allows an earthbound perception and thinking to be set aside. Then you can explore all the possibilities that are opening up to you with this new lens.

Alternatively, your old man creates a siege mentality that resists newness of life, a new identity, and a different possibility. Your mind becomes a battleground, creating confusion through the old man that does not allow for breakthroughs into a new lifestyle. The stress and strain caused by the old can be very debilitating.

Consequently, the scenario becomes more about alleviating the stress than it does in putting on something new. The old man decides in favor of no change and the tension lifts, giving a false illusion of peace. *Tension does not mean that something is wrong.* It means that something is happening! There can be no movement without tension.

In order to cut your food, you must put tension on the knife. To drink from a cup, your handgrip must create tension or the cup cannot be raised. Beloved, there is always a necessary tension between the old and the new. It tells you that something needs to change and that adjustment is vital.

OUTCOMES

Life lived in the old man changes nothing. Any gain that comes from your own performance will never lift you high enough to see the fullness of My perspective of you. Breakthroughs gained in the same way are seldom permanent. There is no lasting breakthrough without the follow-through of establishing a new lifestyle.

Beloved, you cannot hear truth when you are listening to a distortion. You must come aside like Nicodemus and enquire of Me. This is your moment of transformation. There will be many hundreds of wonderful adjustments, some simple, others that require a higher fellowship with Us.

It's the process of how you engage with Me during the change that makes you rich, not just the outcome of becoming different. All learning and change are relational. It is where you receive My love, kindness, affection, mercy, and grace.

The implications for Me are wonderful! I love your process. It is where our joint story merge together as I take you on the journey into My Presence, fullness, and abundance. I love to use all of your life situations as your training ground. I love to teach you how to walk with Me. I cherish those moments when you open your heart as you learn to let go and trust. My affection for you is huge! I treasure the lens by which you learn to see Me, My kingdom, and your place in it.

Everything begins by seeing something. *Are you ready for a lens change?*

INTRODUCTION TO DEEPENING YOUR RESPONSE

The questions in "Deepening Your Response" are a catalyst to your growth—not a quiz. God pursues everything through relationship, trust, vision, imagination, creativity, faith, and His unchanging nature. The questions here are designed to do the same, so they are worded as if God were asking them.

Before You Start:

- Get a journal or small notebook.

- Review Preparing for a Divine Conversation on page 13.

- Start with any question that captivates you. Allow Him to set the pace and order.

- Your first thoughts are an "X" that marks the spot. Return to these questions periodically to dig deeper.

- Your responses should be as expansive as what you are discovering in God.

- Spend as long as you like on any question. Completion is not the goal. Discovering the joy of the journey is. Experience God's delight in being with you in these questions.

- Life is a process, so you will return to these questions again and again—hopefully at a higher level each time. If your learning does not become your lifestyle in Jesus, enjoy cycling through the questions again.

- Embrace the opportunities for relational encounter with Him. They will become your Evidences of Transformation.

- Record your responses in any way that works for you. Love the learning. This is your journey and story with God.

DEEPENING MY RESPONSE TO LETTER 1

"We have a unique perspective about everything We have created."

1. What unique parts of your life do you think I am celebrating?

2. What would change for you if you joined Me?

3. What areas of your life are you comparing to other people's that I am not? Make a list.

4. For each of those on your list, ask Me how I'm celebrating you instead. Write that down, too.

"Beloved, the Earth must adjust to Heaven and its spiritual laws: the law of love, the law of liberty, the law of the Spirit of life in Christ Jesus, to name a few."

A key part of your newness advantage is having New Testament laws! Consider the law of love. According to 1 Corinthians 13, I am legally bound to always be patient with you, always kind, to think no evil, to bear, to believe, and to hope all things. To never fail!

1. Think of a current circumstance in which you would like to feel more confident. Based on this law, how am I thinking about you in that situation?

2. Read 1 Corinthians 13:4-7 as My promise of who I will be for you. In what ways is My perfect law of love overcoming any fears or uncertainties inside your heart?

"Moses desperately wanted Me to see and relate to him in the same way he saw himself.... I knew exactly who Moses was without Me. He needed to understand who he could become with Me."

When was the last time you tried to explain to Me who you were not—or why the circumstances were too hard? See yourself standing with Me in those same circumstances.

1. What is My response to your weakness?

2. Write a short description of who you see yourself to be with Me in this situation now.

"Most people want new but think old. The natural mind can only change when it sees something different. First put off the old, then you are free enough to receive the mind of Christ."

1. Describe one new thing you are seeing differently.

2. What old thought will you choose to set aside to make room for it?

3. How do you think I respond to tension between your old and new thoughts?

"It's the process of how you engage with Me during the change that makes you rich, not just the outcome of becoming different. All learning and change are relational. It is where you receive My love, kindness, affection, mercy, and grace."

1. Describe how this way of learning is different than an academic course of study.

2. What riches are you looking to find with Me along the way?

3. What is the outcome you are hoping for in our relationship? In your development?

"I love to use all of your life situations as your training ground."

1. Where have I created training grounds in your life?

2. What do you suspect that am I training you in?

3. Who do I want to be for you on this practice ground that I couldn't be at any other time?

4. Who are you excited to become through these experiences?

INVITATION TO RESPOND
Are You Ready for a Lens Change?

I've written you a letter, now I'd love to have one from you. I adore your process. It is where our joint stories merge together as I take you on the journey into My Presence, fullness, and abundance.

What do you want to see more clearly about Me? About yourself?

LETTER 2

Unlearning Is the Key to Effective Learning

KEY SCRIPTURES:

Matthew 5; Acts 1:1-8, 2:12 2:37 & 9-10, & 11:1-8; Luke 5:36;

John 3:1-11, 8:34, 16:1-15; Galatians 1:15-18;

Colossians 3:1-3; Hebrews 8:13

Beloved,

When I walked among humans and experienced Old Testament culture and customs, My intention was to introduce a totally new covenant that would make the old one obsolete. I came saying, "You have heard it said, but now I say!" I came to move My people from a visitational culture to a place of abiding in Me and I in them, which is a habitational lifestyle. These two could not possibly be any more different. Like night and day. Like trying to put a new piece of cloth onto an old garment.

THE GOSPELS HIGHLIGHT THE RESISTANCE TO THE NEW

When you read My Gospels, you can understand that they reveal a massive transition to a totally new place of transformation. Newness of life in the new covenant means a complete change—from visitation to habitation, from law to grace, from focus on behavior to engagement with identity, from performance to being accepted, just to name a few!

I am moving you from an external to an internal relationship. From academic study of Scripture to relational theology where experience and encounter with Me are the essence of knowing the truth. When the truth becomes your way of living and sets you free to know and live with Me, then you are free indeed!

The Gospels are as much about unlearning as they are about anything. My clash with religious legalistic people, who had a love of the Law but could not grasp the law of love as a lifestyle, was a continual problem. The constant harassment, judgment, and trick questions of angry Pharisees who only saw Me as a heretic continued for many years—even *after* My resurrection they continued to harass and persecute My followers.

It is still that same religious spirit around today. It is the arrogance of worldly educational knowledge combined with little current Kingdom experience and an inability to learn the difference! When My people do not set their minds on things above, they automatically think from the lower level that is of Earth.

When encountering a new culture, environment, or truth, you stand at a crossroads between what you know, what you *think* you know, and what you could learn *next*. The Flat Earth Society was so amusing to Us because We knew We had made Earth round! Those Society members thought they knew Earth was flat, yet they had a future opportunity to learn something radically new.

I loved My conversation with Nicodemus, who came to talk to Me at night. His academic learning had not prepared him for an encounter with God in a new way. He was a great teacher of something that was passing away. Kingdom learning must always include testimony. Believers teach what they know and testify of what they have seen and experienced. A culture that does not provide experience and encounter cannot represent the Kingdom effectively.

LOVE THE LEARNING

The most important thing to understand, Beloved, is that you must always love the learning that is involved in growing and changing. Uploading truth from the soul (mind, emotions, and will) to your spirit is a marvelous upgrade. From natural to spiritual. From new birth to new man. The learning and unlearning is huge! That is why We gave you the Holy Spirit to lead you into *all* truth.

I love teaching and mentoring you! I am totally enthusiastic about wisdom and revelation. What I'm teaching you, I also cause you to experience. I open up permission for you to encounter Us. There is so much more for you to see, know, and experience!

Every relationship grows through many layers and levels of seeing, thinking, experiencing, and growing. You are learning all the time. Casual acquaintance is vastly different from deep friendship. Courtship to marriage is a shock involving lots of unlearning. Becoming a parent dramatically shifts a lifestyle. Moving through the levels from a toddler to a senior adult provides an astonishing growth spectrum. Why should growing up into all things in Christ be any different?

CONFUSION IS ROOTED IN UNLEARNING

When I showed Peter the vision of a sheet lowered from Heaven with all the non-kosher food, I knew his unlearning would be huge. When I commanded him to eat, he was respectful but resistant, "By no means, Lord, for I have never eaten anything unholy and unclean." How We smiled. Our dear Peter, trying to subtly tell Us We were out of order!

We had to be firm but kind with him, because the stakes here were very high. We wanted to open up the whole gentile world to Heaven. The house of Cornelius was Our pilot project. We explained to Peter, "What God has cleansed, no longer consider unholy."

This was such a huge change, We needed to introduce the concept in stages. First, the idea that something traditionally called "unclean" could now be thought about in a fresh way. Secondly, We needed to introduce him to some gentiles so he could walk with them to another city, which in itself meant having some fellowship on the way. Thirdly, We wanted him to step across the threshold into a gentile home and speak of his faith and love.

He went perplexed. We are never the author of anyone's confusion. Tradition, culture, preconceived ideas, even prejudice, are some of the causes of confusion. But failure to *un*learn is perhaps the greatest cause because it prevents up-to-date learning and is a barrier to growth.

Peter had three years of walking with Me. He heard every message, saw numerous miracles, and was part of the constant dialogue of spiritual things. He spent many of the forty days with Me after My resurrection where I spoke at length about the Kingdom. Yet now, at the house of Cornelius, he had misgivings about My request.

On the way to the home of this gentile, Peter worked some of it out. On arriving he told them his old lens and also what he had unlearned: "You yourselves know how unlawful it is for a man who is a Jew to associate with a foreigner or to visit him; and yet God has shown me that I should not call any man unholy or unclean." I was so proud of him!

Some of the things I am asking My people to unlearn will be huge for them. That is why I am requesting that people approach the truth like a Berean and not like a Pharisee. Bereans were noble-minded, loved truth, and eagerly examined the Scriptures to see if what they were hearing was the truth. Pharisees examined Scripture to prove something wrong and themselves right. It's impossible to learn anything when you start from a negative.

Peter navigated his way to the truth through his love of Me: "I most certainly understand now that God is not one to show partiality, but in every nation the man who fears Him and does what is right is welcome to Him."

I loved that moment! All of Heaven watches these defining moments, where everything changes. Our wonderful Holy Spirit was so excited He could not wait for Peter to finish speaking. He saturated everyone with His Presence to the amazement of all!

ACCELERATING YOUR GROWTH

Learning about the Kingdom is critical. The failure of My people to understand the realm that We operate from is perhaps the biggest obstacle to a revival lifestyle, preventing the world from experiencing the fullness of redemption.

To actually receive the Kingdom you must unlearn the ways of the world and any religious, legalistic interaction with it. To be free means to be pure, joyful, loving, and wholesome. Some believers rail against the world instead of loving and revealing the Kingdom.

Unless you know what you are unlearning, there will be a conflict between your knowledge of Me and your experience of My Presence. Saul, an academic theologian, a Pharisee from one of the strictest legalistic religious sects, genuinely thought he was 100% serving Me by persecuting the church. His rage was incandescent.

His murderous intent was out of control. He was pitiless, a man without mercy.

I showed Him what mercy was like when he encountered Me on the road to Damascus. His perspective of love, grace, and My kindness was so shrouded and dark, when the light of My love touched him, it was so powerful it took his eyesight. People don't realize how blind they are until the light comes.

I sat with Saul for three days, silent, as he was overcome with the confusion and religious turmoil of missing the Messiah's coming, plus the horror of what he had perpetrated in Our name. My heart went out to him in his terror and apprehension. I loved how his story and journey unfolded when the scales fell from his eyes. The obedience of Ananias was so thrilling to Me as he laid hands on Saul to receive his sight and be filled with Me.

My favorite part of his journey? Having him all to Myself in the wilderness for several years as we retraced his steps through Scripture. The Bible is so different when you read it *with* the Author and study it *with* the Creator. Our dialogue was huge as he unplugged from his prejudice and *un*learned his preconceptions.

YOUR LIFE IS OUR ADVENTURE TOO

If the truth has *not* set you free, you must find the lie that binds you. What is your current blockage to really knowing and walking with Me? Why are your dreams about Me greater than your present experience? When was the last time you felt My Presence? What is your personal testimony of the Good News? What three words would best describe your current relationship with Me?

Lack of answers tells you where your story and journey with Me need to change. Beloved, I cherish your learning and I am totally excited about what you will unlearn in the process. Blockages will be destroyed and log jams swept away. So many miracles happened around Saul in his unlearning, and spiritual growth enabled him to transform into Paul the apostle of grace. I adored his metamorphosis just like I will relish your transformation in the new man.

I am with you. I am for you. I am training you. I am making you in Our image. In this process of change, ask questions and wait patiently, trusting Me for the answer. Set time aside and you will know My loving Presence guiding you. Your freedom and growth are Our adventure, too.

My two favorite questions, both asked on the day of Pentecost were: "What does this mean?" and "What must I do?" The first is a relational question. How does this situation affect the quality of our relationship? Remember everything with Us is relational. That's Our priority. The second question is about how you partner together with Me for your upgrade and increase. You must expect Me to accelerate your learning and growth. We have to make up for lost time. Unlearning means you must formally reject the lie that has held you back and slowed down your transformation.

I want you to discover Me and what I am really, really like! In the process you will discover yourself in My affection and grace. If you have been brought up to believe that I am angry at behavior, you will need a revelation and several experiences with My kindness. I'm happy to oblige! If you think that favor is linked to your performance as a believer, you will discover that My favor is because of your placement in Jesus!

I am so looking forward to elevating your lifestyle. The old man has all the stress and struggle. The new man has all the joy and peace in believing. I have no greater joy than to see you learning who I am for you and how you can live immersed in Christ.

I had Jesus take away the sins of the world so that I would not need to be sin-conscious and, therefore, could only focus on righteousness. And that righteousness is Our gift to you—it cannot be earned—it must simply be received. Everything you need Us to be is Our gift to you. Your life is truly marked by what you receive from Us. The prodigal son received everything as a gift. The son who stayed received less because he tried to earn it.

I have so many wonderful things to say to you and some brilliant things to give you. We will do everything together. I will never leave nor forsake you.

Are you ready for an adventure in unlearning?

DEEPENING MY RESPONSE TO LETTER 2

"I came to move My people from a visitational culture to a place of abiding in Me and I in them, which is a habitational lifestyle."

On the cross, Jesus gave Me back My dream of having a perfect relationship with My people. Now, nothing can ever separate you from who I am for you!

1. Make a list of times when you wondered if I was really present.

2. Use this list to write your own version of "Nothing can separate me from You. Not ____, nor _____..."
    Read it aloud every day for several days or weeks.

3. Where did you discover "visitational" mindsets in your expectations of Us?

4. How do you see these now?

5. Share your testimony with Me (and maybe a few others).

"I loved My conversation with Nicodemus who came to talk to Me at night. His academic learning had not prepared him for an encounter with God in a new way."

1. Read My chat with Nicodemus in John 3:1-17. Hear My affection for him in the exchange. Imagine My smile as his previous learning collided with what I was saying.

2. Like Nicodemus, what are some of the sincere questions you have for Me about your newness advantage?

3. What previous learning or traditions are being challenged?

4. Imagine sitting down with Us to discuss these. Describe what that exchange might sound like to you.

"The most important thing to understand, Beloved, is that you must always love the learning that is involved in growing and changing."

1. What are you most excited about learning with Me?

2. What do you think I am most excited to teach you?

3. How would you like Me to be your Helper in that process?

"Bereans were noble-minded, loved truth, and eagerly examined the Scriptures to see if what they were hearing was the truth. Pharisees examined Scripture to prove something wrong and themselves right. It's impossible to learn anything when you start from a negative."

1. How would you describe your starting point as you consider your newness advantage?

2. Of the Scriptures listed at the beginning of this letter, what is one verse that you're seeing in a new way?

"Unless you know what you are unlearning, there will be a conflict between your knowledge of Me and your experience of My Presence."

1. Make a list of new thoughts you're encountering as you read.

2. For each, discover a previously learned truth or tradition that needs to be unlearned.

3. What aspect of My true nature do I want you to experience for each of these?

4. What new encounter(s) with Me are you looking forward to the most?

"If the truth has *not* set you free, you must find the lie that binds you."

Consider the questions that I'm asking you in this letter:

1. What is your current blockage to really knowing and walking with Me?

2. Why are your dreams about Me greater than your present experience?

3. When was the last time you felt My Presence?

4. What is your current testimony of the Good News?

5. What three words would best describe your current relationship with Me?

6. Based on your answers to these, how would you describe our current relationship?

"Beloved, I cherish your learning and I am totally excited about what you will unlearn in the process."

1. Dear one, what have you believed about Me that isn't really the truth?

2. What truth about Me am I excited to have you discover instead?

3. How would you like to partner with Me in your learning and unlearning adventure?

INVITATION TO RESPOND

Dreaming Together

What do you dream of your life with Me being like? What kind of relationship do you long to have? Write Me a letter about it—then listen for My response as I share My dream of the life I already see with you.

LETTER 3

Surrendering to Greatness:
Living the Lifestyle We Create

KEY SCRIPTURES:

Genesis 1:26; Isaiah 54:17; Amos 3:3; Matthew 11:25-30;

John 14:9, 15:1-11, 17:18-25; Romans 6:16-19, 8:37;

1 Corinthians 1:30; 2 Corinthians 5:17, 12:9; Galatians 4:1-7;

Ephesians 1:4-5, 4:1-3, 4:15-24; Philippians 1:27, 4:4; Colossians 1:13;

Titus 2:11-12; 2 Peter 1:4; Revelation 21:5

Beloved,

When you walk with Us you must live the life that We live. That is what it means for you to be made into Our image. There is no duality here. There are not two lives trying to connect. There is one life. Christ in you and you in Christ.

Christ in you provides you with all the same privileges as My Son Himself possesses. You have the same grace, love, power, and capacity in all things. You have His perspective, mindset, and language. We hold nothing back!

You in Christ means that all the earthly situations you encounter come with a predetermined disposition that allows you to expect great things from Us and positions you to receive when you are under pressure. Even on your worst and weakest day you can prosper from being in Jesus. Your life in Christ therefore is about surrendering to Our greatness. It is about resting and learning to relax into Our way of being, and knowing that no weapon fashioned against you can prosper.

Christ in you is concerned with His lordship reigning and ruling regardless of your circumstances. *You in Christ* is bowing to His lordship and accepting His rule in your weakness. A perfect partnership that means when you are weak, you are also strong!

PLACEMENT AND PORTRAYAL

Christ in you and *you in Christ* are best described in two words: placement and portrayal.

Placement means that by Our doing, you are in Christ Jesus. We chose you long before you met Us. We had a plan for you before your birth. We chose you to become Our child, Our heir in the fullness of Jesus. Our delight is to love you the same way as We love Him. It is vitally important for Us that you become the Beloved. In Him, you have been transferred to the Kingdom of the Beloved One, Jesus. We do not take this lightly. It is the very heart of Our fellowship with you.

Placement is where you have permission to recognize that We have put you into a very specific position as a gift from Us. You can do nothing to enter this place—it is a gift. You must do everything to remain and live in this place—it is called abiding.

Portrayal makes the art of abiding a new lifestyle. This is where you learn to represent this Kingdom-life here on Earth. All your life issues and circumstances are about you learning to draw from all that We are in you, to you, and through you. It is where you learn the pleasure of representing the King and His Kingdom.

As chosen ones you put on the same nature and character that We possess. You represent goodness, kindness, compassion, gentleness, and humility. Our nature becomes your lifestyle. You learn to take great delight in walking in a manner worthy of My indwelling Presence in your life. Your real-life situations are the classroom where I empower you to become like Us.

Powerful believers do not look for rescue in their circumstances. They look for majesty. They expect to find Us joyfully providing and working powerfully. We love your life as We love Our own, because it is the same! We are one in Christ Jesus.

Jesus said to His disciples, "If you have seen Me, then you have seen the Father." His placement on Earth was to be the Messiah, the Deliverer, the Savior. His portrayal of the nature of God was the evidence that He was sent from Heaven. He constantly referred to Me, the One who had sent Him, and He did My will above all else.

You, too, are now sent in His name to do the same things: to rise up and overcome all obstacles just as He would; to portray His life in the midst of your own weakness. *Portrayal* means you identify with His gift of life and, therefore, in the Holy Spirit you can provide evidence of who He is for you.

SECURE IN OUR LOVE

We start with you at your weakest point—a born-again child—and We gradually empower and elevate you to a place of full sonship. We teach you to rest so that you do not live weary or burdened. We demonstrate and empower you through the joy of partnership—a shared yoke. We teach you the majesty of Our strength. Nothing is too hard for Us. You are not a difficult proposition, Beloved!

It is vital that in your placement training you learn to be secure in Our love. Your needs will be met as you learn to rest and trust. The world is difficult, Beloved, but the Kingdom is not! The way to live from Kingdom to Earth is to practice with Us the joy and peace in believing.

To have Me *in* you means that you are learning to live in and from a place of the Father's delight in you. You are constantly discovering Our goodness and how to be constantly refreshed by My Presence in you. Goodness is one of the most compelling of lifestyles.

You must also experience grace as Our empowering Presence that enables you to become the person that We see in Me. All your learning is covered by grace. All your mistakes are covered even before you make them. That is the grace of empowered Presence that is Me in you, an expectation of something amazing that is happening. Embrace the certainty of who We are for you.

You are learning to be accepted in the Beloved. As you receive Christ, so you walk in Him. You will experience the joy and wonder of being in Christ. The same oneness that Jesus had with the Father, you may have in Him, as you learn to let Us love you. You are learning a necessary, thrilling dependency that will last a lifetime. The life We create, for you and in you, is one of enjoyment. It is a celebratory lifestyle marked by rejoicing, thanksgiving, and gratitude.

LEARNING THE LANGUAGE OF YOUR TRUE IDENTITY

This is why, Beloved, you must learn the language of the new man in Christ. The speech of the old you is inappropriate for the life We have set aside for you. As a believer, living in newness of spirit and operating in newness of life, you must stop giving away your advantage in Jesus. In your placement you are learning in all your life issues to see differently and to engage with the mind of Christ. New thinking creates new language, which is evidence of your growth and development in the Kingdom.

You are a new creation, My Love. All the old has passed away; I make everything new in Christ. This is My gift to you, available forever, starting now! If you do not learn the perspective, thinking, and language of the new man, then your experience of Me can never rise to the full level available in the Kingdom. You will have victories but you will not be an overcomer. You will win some battles but you will not become more than a conqueror. This is an existence, but not the life Jesus was dying to give you.

Learning the ways of the new man gives you power to become an adult son or daughter of God and take on the spirit and character of Jesus. Only in Him can you escape the viewpoint, thinking, and conversation of the world around you. Wanting new but thinking old is classic futility. We want you to enjoy being with Us, to love the everyday learning of practicing the lifestyle of Heaven.

Learning how to put off the old habits and put on new characteristics is a gloriously enjoyable daily upgrade of identity. There is so much for you to receive. You cannot avoid any of the development We have planned for your continuous upgrade when you are abiding in Me. If you bob and weave in and out of your old man, you can choose to delay your transformation, even postpone it for a season, but you cannot cancel it. If you *remain* living in your old man, you may talk yourself out of favor, power, and the sonship experience until your dying day. You may never allow yourself the life We want you to have. In that case, you will never have walked with Us effectively and Our reality will not have existed for you. However, by living in a state of reciprocal abiding with Me, it is impossible to miss out on the upgrades that accompany the identity you are stepping into.

Knowing your placement and what you can portray at each stage of your story and journey guarantees an ongoing blessing and favor in your life. You will be introduced to the perspective of increase—more and greater fullness! This is where you grow in praise, thanksgiving, and rejoicing as an instinctive outburst of gratitude. There is a place where you may think through your rejoicing so that you learn to live as a celebrant. Worship is often the impulse within you that is generated from Our delight in you!

Praise at its most intuitive and visceral occurs because it is inherent in the Spirit that indwells you. That is how you can learn to rejoice always, and again I say rejoice! The indwelling Presence pulls worship out of you as you practice being a delighted child.

YOUR INHERITANCE IS AT STAKE

As you are growing up into Christ in all things, you may also practice the lifestyle of a joint heir with Christ. Because He is in you, the same privilege, favor, and provision that He enjoys now also are available to you. Being young in Christ is not related to how many years you have been a believer. It is connected to your experience of Him in various areas of life. A person can be in Christ for forty years but have the spiritual experience of a small child. When your mental knowledge of Christ is greater than your experience of Me, you will be living below His means in your life. That is like living the best life possible in Egypt when the Promised Land is freely available. Knowledge that does not lead to encounters and experiences of the Christ cannot empower you to become like Us.

As a child of God you are an heir. Even at your weakest and young-est state, you are already a beneficiary and an inheritor in life. This is vital to grasp. Your guardian and manager of your estate is the incredible Holy Spirit. He will not only teach you how to get your needs met but also how to understand the power and privilege of being in Me.

Beloved, I long for you to learn the favor that comes from your placement in Me and how to live that out through the incompa-rable Holy Spirit who teaches you to ask and believe. You own everything as an heir of fullness. You need the lifestyle that goes with that revelation. Each stage of your life is therefore about trusting and being trusted.

NEW THINKING PRODUCES NEW LEVELS OF ENCOUNTER

One of the signs of your growing up in Christ is that you know the truth and it has set you free by your actual experience to be-come new. The new man in Christ must be seen, heard, and en-countered. You must not become vulnerable to religious doctrines that remove the freedoms that Jesus died to release to you.

We know that you are growing up in Christ when your thinking takes you to new levels of encounter within the Kingdom. You develop your spirit to have a more powerful way of engaging with Christ from within. At the same time, you retain that wonderful simple way of saying "No!" to any ill will, any vindictive, angry, ungracious, unkind behavior that produces a bitter, futile lifestyle.

All the key elements of self-worth are the outcome of being in Christ. The evidence of those outcomes occurs most naturally as you engage with Me to make war on all your negativity. The truth that sets you free is all about how We see you in Christ. The new-man lifestyle is essential and mandatory if you want to grow up into Him in all things. Your identity from a beloved child to fully mature adult depends on the new man. If that ongoing maturation process is not occurring, you cannot become all that We desire.

Visualize your lifestyle through the language that We are using to describe how We see you! An unstable person is always in two minds, tossed here and there in life. If you see yourself as a sinner but We see you as a saint, one of us has the wrong picture.

If you are trying to change your behavior without developing your identity in the new man first, you will have a disconnect with Our primary purpose of **"Let Us make man in Our image."** The principle is that you do not become a new person by changing your behavior. You discover your identity in Christ and act accordingly. It is called being renewed in the spirit of your mind. Only the new man has renewed thinking that changes everything.

AGREEMENT WITH HEAVEN EMPOWERS YOU ON EARTH

When your perception does not agree with Our view of you, then you cannot walk with Us properly as We desire. It becomes more difficult in that context for you to receive what We want to give. Can two walk together unless they are agreed?

The mind of a sinner can receive forgiveness but still live under the shadow of guilt and condemnation. A sinner mindset dwells on failings and shortcomings. It looks at personal faults and internalizes shame. Life is an endless round of seeking forgiveness for the same things because the old man cannot change. Only the new man can grow up fully in Me.

Beloved, you were a sinner who has been saved by the grace of empowering Presence to become a saint. No longer a sinner, you are learning to walk in newness of life, as a child of light, as the beloved of God, and as My heir. It is impossible to be fully aware of Me within you and still live a mediocre lifestyle. In Me, the new man has a new nature. You do not have a sin nature; you have a sin habit that We are delighted to help you break by using the gift of righteousness.

When you submit to guilt and shame, it is because you are listening to the enemy and stepping back into the performance mentality of your old man. A lifestyle that only practices avoidance of sin will constantly engage with sin to its own detriment. What you focus on, you empower. We are not sin-conscious because Jesus dealt with sin once and for all!

A sin-conscious lifestyle will question your identity in Jesus. The gospel of glad tidings will not work effectively because you are believing something contrary to Our Word and integrity. A sinner mindset produces a language that releases a negative. It's the language of doubt, lies, unbelief, fear, anxiety, and low self-esteem that will ensure that you will not experience Our fullness.

When you present yourself in the old man, you are a slave of obedience to the nature that governs that lifestyle. When you present yourself as dead to the old and alive to the new man in Christ, you partake of the true nature of God. In the new man in Jesus, your perspective and thinking transform your language to reflect Our heart for you.

The new man, literally the saint, is a person who is delighted in God and occupied fully with who Jesus is. The old has gone and the new man is reveling in being a new creation. My question to you is, which self is talking? The old or the new? And which one are you going to listen to?

The new man releases a new spirit, heart, mind, lens, voice, language, lifestyle, person, and creation.

What is your new man saying about you?

DEEPENING MY RESPONSE TO LETTER 3

"Your life in Christ… is about surrendering to Our greatness."

1. Beloved, what has a surrendered life looked like for you before now?

2. How would your perceptions and thinking change if you thought of "surrender" like I do?

"Placement is where you have permission to recognize that We have put you into a very specific position as a gift from Us. You can do nothing to enter this place—it is a gift."

I celebrate your placement in Christ with the gift of My Presence. Some days I will be present to your feelings, some days to your faith, but I am always present. Come sit with Me as you and I discuss these things.

1. What do you have for Me to receive today?

2. What am I expecting to receive?

3. Tell Me about it. Write a few notes. I'd love to hear.

"Powerful believers do not look for rescue in their circumstances. They look for majesty. They expect to find Us joyfully providing and working powerfully."

1. Think of a current challenging life situation. Look around. Where am I standing in it?

2. What provision do I have for you to receive?

3. What weakness of yours will you exchange for My strength?

4. How is this situation a classroom for practicing your placement in Me?

5. How will you portray Me to others in this circumstance?

"Jesus said to His disciples, 'If you have seen Me, you have seen the Father....' You, too, are now sent in His name to do the same things. To rise up and overcome all obstacles just as He would. To portray His life in the midst of your weakness."

1. When people encounter you, what do you want them to encounter of Me?

"All your learning is covered by grace. All your mistakes are covered even before you make them."

1. If this is true (and with Me, it is!), what are you now willing to attempt?

2. What new freedoms does this thought unlock for you?

3. What previous anxieties does My grace lock up? Make a list.

4. What are you learning right now that I am rejoicing to see?

"As a believer, living in newness of spirit and operating in newness of life, you must stop giving away your advantage in Jesus."

1. Beloved, where have you given away your advantage in Me?

2. Imagine Me coming to you with My arms full of what you once thought was lost. What rises in your heart as you see Me walking towards you?

3. What would you like to receive back that I've held on to?

"All the key elements of self-worth are the outcome of being in Christ."

1. When I look at your life in Me, what do I see?

2. Where would you like to see your life through My eyes?

3. What new confidence rises as you look through My lens?

"The principle is that you do not become a new person by changing your behavior. You discover your identity in Christ and act accordingly."

1. What does that truth set you free from?

2. What new identity in Me are you discovering?

3. What would change in your behavior to reflect that?

"When you submit to guilt and shame, it is because you are listening to the enemy and stepping back into the performance mentality of your old man... The new man is delighted in God and occupied fully with who Jesus is."

1. What type of thoughts most occupy how you think about yourself?

2. How do I think about you?

3. Which thoughts about yourself do you want to consider most? Mine or yours? Make a list.

INVITATION TO RESPOND
Portrayal

How will you portray Me throughout your lifetime? Write Me a letter that shares who you hope to become in Me and who you desire to impact with My goodness.

LETTER 4

Grace that Overcomes

Beloved,

The language that We use in talking about grace tells you the magnitude of what it means to Us on a personal level. When Moses asked Me to show him My glory, I spoke to him about My goodness. His shocked face was a picture—it made Me smile. He was not ready for that concept. To Me though, it is impossible for goodness not to be glorious, amazing, all sufficient, and dominating.

I love to lavish My goodness upon you. My goodness encompasses My grace, which is My empowering Presence that enables you to become the person that I see when I look at you! The abundance of grace will shape the way that you see Me, yourself, and others.

It will provoke you to love and kindness. In this way, the pattern of grace and glory combining can be set and established through your life circumstances. If grace elevates your relationship with Me, it cannot be used to downgrade that same relationship.

GRACE PLUS RIGHTEOUSNESS

The abundance of grace overcomes all the consequences of transgression, condemnation, disobedience, and death. Sin entered the world through one man's transgression, spreading sin and death to everyone. If by that one transgression all could die, how much more will the abundance of grace and the gift of righteousness abound to all who embrace the righteous One? Grace is *so* much more powerful than sin. Judgment came from one single transgression, resulting in widespread condemnation for all. However, the free gift of righteousness paired with copious grace was the outcome of one Man's obedience that resulted in justification for everyone.

The difference, Beloved, is not just that grace is consistently more powerful in itself. It is that the abundance of grace, together with the gift of righteousness, will elevate you to a higher place of relationship with Me. This means that grace and righteousness allow you to reign in all your circumstances *in the same way* as the One, Jesus Christ.

Most people only connect grace to sin. They minimize grace in order not to minimize unrighteousness. But when you combine My gift of grace with My gift of righteousness, a ruling power emerges in your life causing you to rise up to a new place of relationship and fellowship with Me. Because of the obedience of My beloved Son, you also can be made righteous.

That is why when sin increases, grace always increases, too, so that it continues reigning! Grace rules through righteousness. Sin has already been dealt with once and for all on the cross. So, the real question is this: How can you, who in Christ have died to sin, ever live in it, when you are alive to Me in Christ?

His death governs your behavior so that grace and righteousness together can establish your identity in newness of life in Christ. I love your identity! My Son paid a hefty price for your freedom. And We all agree—*you are worth it!*

Grace controls and directs all the negatives into a place where they are utterly defeated and must turn into something that is totally opposite. The power of grace and the supremacy of righteousness when integrated into your circumstances will lift you into a holiness that will be remarkable to you.

THE NEWNESS ADVANTAGE

Beloved, you do not start this newness of life as a disadvantaged person. Everything in your old life has been killed off. It has been taken away and buried. You have risen up in newness of life and been given a *brand new* identity. Christ in you is the new man coming through in all your circumstance. You have amazing grace as you learn the fullness of this new nature. Jesus dealt with your sin. I am establishing your righteousness on the same ground of grace that rules over sin. This is a divine advantage!

In this life, you are now learning the grace of overcoming. I am teaching you to prevail and triumph in the way of righteousness. You are not helpless; you have power. You are not defenseless; you are secure in the One. As He is, so are you! The newness advantage means you never start each day with a deficit. You start with sufficiency.

Grace creates more than enough to empower you to rise up and overcome. What We give you is legally sufficient. Grace is a ruling power that creates the opposite of what legalism intends. You can always tell when a religious spirit is speaking. It will always downgrade the power and effectiveness of grace. The enemy calls it cheap grace because he wants to keep you poor both in goodness received and favor bestowed.

In grace, Jesus became poor so that you might become rich in His identity. Grace rules because Christ in you is righteous and you partake of His divine nature. The beauty and majesty of His life within cause grace to reign. I ask you, Beloved, how would grace reign over guilt, shame, or condemnation?

As part of your development in grace and upgrade in righteousness, how would grace as empowering Presence dominate the negative opinions of people who do not apply grace even to themselves? This is a good dialogue for you to have with Me. When you stand in grace before the throne of grace, the majesty of My empowering Presence will liberate you into freedom. It will rise up and occupy your heart.

A humility will rise with it that will allow you to think about yourself with a sound assessment. You should think highly of yourself because you are in Christ. There is no value in denigrating yourself. I do not require you to be negative about yourself. It does not glorify Me and sounds strange. I am giving you a measure of faith to see yourself in Christ. Humility promotes a gratitude that allows you to enjoy your elevation without attributing it to your own efforts. Do not think more highly about yourself than you ought to think—but *do* think highly of yourself, please!

AUTHORITY IN GRACE

Grace is sufficient for *every* eventuality. I will always supply enough of what is most essential. Your sufficiency is My responsibility. Your authority in grace comes from My permission for you to "consider yourself dead to sin and be alive to Me in Christ." Grace provides you with plenty of power to stand before Me content with My Presence and with power to respond to the Holy Spirit in what He is cultivating in you.

I love to make grace, My ruling power, abound to the new man. Then you can practice the overflow lifestyle necessary to allow your new man to come to the fore in Jesus. Power is always perfected in weakness when grace is present in your life situation. Your dependence on grace creates contentment that counteracts any negative perspective, mindset, or language. Grace produces strength in the weakest places of your experience in goodness. Grace raises a barrier against any negative predicament so that weakness, distress, persecution, and difficulties do not overwhelm you. In Christ We are creating you to be like Us—strong, joyful, loving, and kind with the strength to overcome.

It is not honoring to Us when you can only see yourself as deficient, inadequate, poor in spirit, with meagre resources. All your supply in the Spirit comes to Christ in you. He is always worthy! You have no lack in your life situation because you can never face them alone. We will never leave you. There is always sufficient power for you to rise up and stand with Us in Our strength.

ACKNOWLEDGING MY PRESENCE

Hold on to your confession of the Jesus who lives in you and who *really* knows you. He is the One who knows you best and loves you the most! His grace in you gives you a massive confidence to trust in the fullness of My heart towards you. His grace must be seen, known, and felt. It must be experienced as something glorious, because grace and glory can never be separated. Love covers a multitude of sins and grace cannot be separated from love. All the language around grace must become as rich as the written Word exemplifies.

Christ in you understands all that you are going through. I use grace to teach you to acknowledge His Presence in a higher way. What you experience in grace will take you into My manifest Presence. Grace covers your present-past lifestyle beautifully and opens you up to the impressive future that belongs to you in Christ. Grace makes you rich in Presence. Beloved, if grace is designed to overwhelm you, then surely it is also designed to overwhelm everything that opposes you!

Grace is not an argument. It is a lifestyle in Christ where you and anyone you meet can encounter goodness, loving kindness, and favor. In this manner, grace compels you in a normal way to walk with God more in the context of the Kingdom than the world. My empowering Presence is stronger than any nuclear power, more influential than any earthly government, and more compelling than any man-made rules.

This is all part of the law of the Spirit of life that is in Me. It contains the law of love and the perfect law of liberty, and it empowers you to do for others what you would want most for yourself. There is a majesty in grace that will overshadow any accusation of the enemy or any legalistic opinions of man.

Grace empowers you to receive mercy. This is Our full and stupendous compassion that authorizes you to find grace to help in time of need. In grace, the Spirit empowers you to overcome your past history by teaching you how to abound in My Presence. I love overwhelming shame, condemnation, and legalistic cynicism. It is time for you to surpass your expectations of My kindness towards you!

STRONG IN GRACE

It is good for your heart to be strengthened by grace. I would love you to be strong in mercy, kindness, love, and goodness. Then you would enjoy Me so much more. I will always want to comfort and strengthen your heart in My goodness. You need to have a positive expectation of My heart towards you.

Abundant grace is the catalyst for you to grow in an accelerated manner in the new man. I want you to have the same testimony of My grace as I do about My character. I always say, "I AM that I AM." I want you to testify, "By the grace of God, I am that I am. His grace has not been in vain."

Grace is the catalyst for confidence and boldness in your fellowship with Me. It is vital for your growth that you develop a powerful attitude of partnering with the grace the Holy Spirit is pouring into you.

When you are in Christ and He is operating in you, then you get to experience life exactly as He does Himself. This is the very definition of Christ in you, the hope (or expectation) of His glory. When circumstances get ugly, this makes grace more beautiful. Grace tells you how you are seen and known by Me. How I relate to you in this situation tells you the type of person I want you to become. Always between seeing and becoming, there lies an acceptance of grace and a learning to live in your available position in Christ.

GRACE EMPOWERS PROCESS

Beloved, if grace is so amazing and powerful, then why do some people try to judge others into a place of change? If grace is about freedom, then you need to be free to process it through the nature of God, not the rules of behavior set by man. When you feel forced to give way to a negative, it is My empowering Presence that is overlooked. You neutralize what I want to be for you when you give no value to grace.

I went to the cross to rob you of all worldly negatives. They have no place in your new nature. Because you are in Me, you are dead to them. Joyfully practice being alive to Me while seeing yourself dead to everything in that old nature. When you are more conscious of sin than you are of My kindness, goodness, grace, and love, then you cannot know the fullness of who I want to be for you. You can only walk at a lower level of identity.

Grace is a ruling power that releases the wonder of My nature and character to you, regardless of your circumstances. You may bring that empowering Presence to any place you like. It will create the opposite of what legalism demands. When grace and righteousness combine in your heart, then you become a partaker of My divine nature.

I love your life and learning. I love who you are now with all your faults and mistakes because I see who you can become. Grace will get you out of a negative so you can encounter all the possibilities because I live in you!

Grace will accelerate your development in who I am for you. I would like to move faster. Momentum in grace is so exciting! Shall we go for a run?

DEEPENING MY RESPONSE TO LETTER 4

"...the abundance of grace, together with the gift of righteousness, will elevate you to a higher place of relationship with Me."

1. What is the experience of abundant, lavish, limitless grace that you would like to step up into?

2. If I'm delighted to give you the gift of righteousness (and I am!), what areas of righteousness are you ready to receive?

3. If you left behind the idea of "good days" and "bad days," how would life change if there were only "days of grace"?

"Grace controls and directs all the negatives into a place where they are utterly defeated and must turn into something that is totally opposite."

1. Take several small squares of paper. On one side, write down a negative you see in your character. (Use a particular color pen for all the negatives.)

2. On the back side of the paper square, write My opposite for your negative. (Use a different color pen for My opposites.)

3. Lay out all your negatives, face up. Try to remember My opposite for one—then flip it! Make it a game. See if you can remember all of My opposites.

4. After playing with Me for a while, turn all My opposites face up. What would your life be like if you only saw My opposites when a negative arose? How fast do you want to learn to "flip it"? And how would your perspective change if you saw this as a game I love to play with you?

5. What is displaced when you fill up on the joy of My opposites?

6. How else could you use this to create delight in flipping negatives?

"Grace rules because Christ in you is righteous and you partake of His divine nature. The beauty and majesty of His life within cause grace to reign. I ask you, Beloved, how would grace reign over guilt, shame, or condemnation?"

1. How would you answer that question? I'd love to hear.

2. What would change in your perceptions, thinking, and language if My grace reigned supreme over all thoughts of shame, guilt, and condemnation?

"...how would grace as empowering Presence dominate the negative opinions of people who do not apply grace even to themselves? This is a good dialogue for you to have with Me. When you stand in grace before the throne of grace, the majesty of My empowering Presence will liberate you into freedom. It will rise up and occupy your heart."

1. Let's begin that dialogue. Think of a current situation where someone has a negative opinion of you. What negative have you believed about yourself that I am not believing about you?

2. See yourself standing confidently in My empowering Presence before My throne of grace. What rises up in your heart towards Me?

3. Who does it liberate you to become that didn't seem possible before?

"There is no value in denigrating yourself. I do not require you to be negative about yourself. It does not glorify Me and sounds strange. I am giving you a measure of faith to see yourself in Christ."

1. If you had the faith of Jesus (and you do!), how would you see yourself as He sees you? What's different?

"Grace is sufficient for every eventuality. I will always supply enough of what is most essential. Your sufficiency is My responsibility."

1. When your sufficiency is My responsibility, what new freedom do you feel?

2. How do you plan to explore and celebrate that new freedom?

"I love to make grace, My ruling power, abound to the new man. Then you can practice the overflow lifestyle necessary to allow your new man to come to the fore in Jesus."

1. What overflow lifestyle would you like to imagine? Write about it.

"Christ in you understands all that you are going through. I use grace to teach you to acknowledge His Presence in a higher way... Grace covers your present-past lifestyle beautifully and opens you up to the impressive future that belongs to you in Christ."

Wherever you are, I've been there, too. Let's look around your circumstances together and discover where I am standing in them. When you see Me, come stand with Me.

1. What is the gift of grace that I have in My hands for you?

2. How am I using it to teach you more of who I really am?

3. When I look into your future, who do I see you becoming?

"Grace is not an argument."

1. If sin abounds, grace will abound even more. So it seems rather silly to argue about the boundaries of grace, doesn't it? Beloved, what boundaries on My grace do you have for yourself and/or others that I don't have?

2. Describe the new revelation of grace that you would like to explore.

3. What new desire for righteousness does this revelation of grace provoke in you?

"When you are more conscious of sin than you are of My kindness, goodness, grace, and love, then you cannot know the fullness of who I want to be for you. You can only walk at a lower level of identity."

1. If your experience of grace were a 100-story building (where *fullness* of grace is the penthouse), what floor are you living on?

2. Describe what that floor looks like. What are the perceptions, mindsets, and language that take up residence there?

3. What key truth(s) about grace do you want to accept that will take you 10 (or 20 or 30) floors higher?

INVITATION TO RESPOND
Grace

"I love your life and your learning. I love who you are now with all your faults and mistakes because I see who you can become. Grace will get you out of a negative so you can encounter all the possibilities because I live in you!"

What is your response to My delight and excitement in all you are learning about grace? Write and tell me what you're discovering about Me, about you, and about how amazing My grace truly is.

LETTER 5

Dying to Self and Having a Wonderful Time

KEY SCRIPTURES:

Matthew 4:4; Luke 4:1-13; John 8:36, 14:6, 15:1-11;

Romans 3:3, 5:10, 5:16-25, 6:1-14, 8:1-14, 8:38, 12:1, 13:14, 14:17, 15:13;

1 Corinthians 15:49; 2 Corinthians 5:17, 9:8; Galatians 2:20, 5:22-23;

Ephesians 1:6, 2:5-10, 4:15; Philippians 2:13; Colossians 2:11-13;

1 Thessalonians 5:10, 5:16-19; 2 Timothy 2:11; Hebrews 10:20, 12:2, 13:8;

James 1:2; 1 Peter 2:24; 1 John 1:4, 4:17-19

Beloved,

Every action of the Holy Spirit in your life is to increase your engagement with the primary purpose of the Kingdom. We want to make you in Our image! We want you to live in the same quality of love that exists between each of Us in the Godhead. In that context, We want you to love your learning and welcome your growth opportunities. Then you can change enough to embrace the *next* thing We want to do for you, in you, and through you.

FROM BEHAVIOR TO IDENTITY

The plan of salvation was to make learning and changing easier by removing the hardest part of the process—you! Obviously, We want you to be as righteous and holy as Ourselves and to enjoy the process of becoming like Us. To do that We needed to take away the problem of a sin nature and create within you the characteristics of a person who loves righteousness.

Jesus has done the hard work of redemption by taking your old man to the cross. He did not just die *for* you, He also died *as* you, so that your old nature would no longer have a place in your new life. Now that Christ is in you, His life in you is filled with the truth of how He is *for* you and *in* you. Now that you also are in Christ, your life is filled with the promise of His lifestyle, favor, and faith. The only small struggle that you have is with a sin habit, not a sin nature. The sin culture of the world has caused you to behave in a predetermined way. Now that you are in the Kingdom, We are refocusing how you live, think, learn, and speak so that transformation happens from the inside out.

I am reprogramming your will to come under the new man rather than resort to the habits of the old. In all your life issues, I am training you to be made in Our image, not to continue in one that is already dead to you. I am changing your focus from behavior to identity. As you grow up in Christ, what changes the way you live is that you become more sharply defined in who you are in Him. Identity is the key to transformation. We've said it before: You do not become a new person by changing your behavior. You discover the person that you *already are* in Jesus and act accordingly.

You are *not* the evidence of death to self. Jesus is the evidence. Did He die as you? When He died, did you die on the cross? When He was buried, who was buried with Him? When He rose again to newness of life, who also rose with Him? Beloved, if your old man rose from the dead, then the sacrifice of My Son would be pointless. Nothing would be changed if it's the same old you in charge of your life. Your life would be the same old struggle with sin. Where would be the newness of life and spirit that would empower you to become like Us as you learn Our lifestyle?

Jesus is the evidence that your old man is dead. We create the new man in you, which means you are being saved by His life. The new man in Christ is always making an agreement with the life within. We are not asking you to sacrifice; Jesus already did that for you! It's not about your effort or struggle to be better. We are asking you to focus on His life and to learn to walk in Him, through Him, as Him, and with Him. His life, righteousness, holiness, grace, faith, character, and power all belong to you.

ALIVE TOGETHER WITH CHRIST

Freedom begins when you consider yourself to be dead and learn to be alive to Me. He who is dead is free. Dead people rest in peace. They do not struggle with life. I give you absolute permission to think of your old man as dead so that your new man can simply practice being alive to Me.

What does that mean? It means to become preoccupied with Me. To give My life the preeminence in all your life situations. It means you are not *in* your old nature trying to move towards a new relationship. Instead you are the new man moving *from* your new relationship and using your current life issues to practice and establish your real identity.

This freedom to be alive to Me is therefore all about Our Presence in you. That means you must live your life the way We live Ours! I am the Way, Truth, and Life. Those three areas of identity are already in the DNA of the new, true you in Me. You are now learning how to live in outrageous love. We live in joy in everything. Our peace is ongoing and never ending. This life was meant to be loved and enjoyed. There simply is no other way to live it.

Being alive to Me means that My way of living life becomes the truth of how you practice My Presence. Enjoy Our Presence as a reality in all your life circumstances. In every life event, the prime issue concerns who you get to become in Me. That is your focus. The resolution of the circumstances will naturally follow an upgrade in identity. The entire process is to be fully enjoyed!

We will enjoy teaching you Our way. We will love you in every step of your transformation. Our grace for you will cover a multitude of errors in learning and becoming. Our peace in you will be relentless in dealing with your stress in the development process. Establishing rest and peace will automatically eliminate stress and struggle.

The key to enjoyment of this lifestyle is the understanding that you are made alive together with Jesus. You cannot be separated from Him and We will never leave you nor forsake you. When you were dead in your transgression on the cross, We made you alive together with Him through grace.

Grace is Our empowering Presence that enables you to become the person that We see in Christ. We have a huge and boundless expectation towards you that is designed to fill you with all Our joy and peace in believing. This creates the same amazing expectation in you by the power of the Holy Spirit. The Kingdom of God in your heart is governed by the righteousness, peace, and joy of the Holy Spirit in you. You can thoroughly enjoy the process of your own transformation in Jesus!

A NEW CREATION LIFESTYLE

Only the enemy wants your focus to be on dying to self by your own efforts. That way he controls your failure and with it your condemnation. Instead of that approach to salvation, We have given you a quickening spirit in Jesus. In Him, you have the same ability to respond immediately to truth and life. You are alert and active in the new man in Christ. You are no longer sluggish and slow. You are aware and invested in life as We see it. You are learning in every situation who We are for you, as you learn to see life from Our perspective.

When you walk in relationship with Us, Our life makes you sensitive to truth, which then compels you to pursue freedom. Your first freedom is that you are dead to sin. Your second freedom is that you are alive to Me and processing events with the joy and peace in believing. What the cross was for Jesus, it cannot be for you. For Him, the cross was pain, anguish, suffering, separation, and death. For you it is joy, peace, freedom, Presence, and life. For the joy set before Him, My Son endured the cross. You, abounding in the joy of His constant Presence, are practicing His life at every opportunity. In the power of the Holy Spirit you are cheerful, energetic, and full of life in Jesus. That is what it means to be alive together with Him.

In the context of you developing this new life, We want you to remember that you are Our workmanship created in Christ Jesus. I love watching you discover what We have already prepared for you to walk in as part of your identity! There are so many good things that you must experience in Jesus as We develop your new man. I am at work in you, giving you the desire and the power to fulfill Our good purposes. As you focus on Our reciprocal joy, you will count all your circumstances as joyful even when they are difficult.

You are Our new creation in Christ. We have ordained that the old you has passed way. Today you have Our blessing and permission to seize the new things that belong to you in Jesus. The way that We have designed for you to process can only be received through rejoicing and thanksgiving in Our plans for you in Christ. Beloved, if you do not pay attention to Our cheerfulness in life, you will quench the capacity of the Holy Spirit in your circumstances.

SHARE IN GOD'S STORY

You are chosen before the foundation of the world to join Our relational community. It is vital that you see yourself connected with the Godhead. Nothing can separate you from Our love. Your joy springs out of a constant fellowship with Us. In that process you will automatically gain freedom by being alive to Us. Mature spirituality is an invitation to share, intermingle, and merge your personal story with Ours. I invite you to join Us so that you may know the dynamic love that is generated by Our mutual life, love, and laughter together.

Our Self-knowledge includes knowledge of you. Our Self-love includes love for you. Once you accept your place in Christ, you must accept the place of love that comes with it. We love you in the same way that We love Jesus, as the Beloved Son! Regardless of how well or poorly you are doing, We love you in the same way We love One Another. In this glorious place of loving fellowship, you are accepted in the Beloved. Your mistakes have a powerful forgiveness attached. Mercy accompanies you in all your learning processes.

This is Our covenant with Jesus. Whoever the Son sets free will indeed be set free. By putting Him into you, and also you into Him, We guarantee that Our love for you will be unchanging—yesterday, today, and forever. Past, present, and future are all covered with love, joy, peace, and grace. You have this constant impartation of life as you are made alive in the fullness of Christ. The same power that raised Him from the dead is now working to elevate His new man in you as you face any situation. We love the classroom of your life circumstances. This is where you learn to bear the image of the heavenly.

As you learn the joyful process of living with Us, your capacity to grow up in all things increases. When your learning flows out of loving Us and being with Us and not attached to any amount of "trying to do the right thing" to please Us, something amazing happens. You automatically experience the results of being crucified with Me and We can't help but rejoice! We rejoice that He lives in you. We rejoice that this life that you now live in Him is by faith. As He is confident in His Sonship, so are you confident in becoming a maturing child who is learning to be His co-heir. We rejoice that grace as empowering Presence will remain with you always.

THE LAW OF THE SPIRIT OF LIFE

In Christ, condemnation is rendered impotent because grace abounds to you. Walking in the law of the Spirit of Life creates a momentum in freedom that automatically brings closure to your old life. The Holy Spirit is now the driving force in your development. He takes everything that belongs to Jesus and empowers your growth in the new man. He is focused on who Jesus is for you. He remains with you through your whole life process of being made in Our image.

As your mind becomes focused on the way that the Holy Spirit works in your life, a peace will overwhelm you. Peace is key to your development simply because learning is more difficult when you allow anxiety and stress to be present. It is the presence of Christ in you that makes your spirit alive to righteous thinking and a righteous lifestyle. He is the same Spirit that raised Jesus from the dead. He will also elevate Christ in you because He abides in you also! Imbedded within Our majesty is the power for you to be made alive in Jesus. As you practice being led by the Spirit, your own sonship and status as a co-heir with Christ carries powerful guarantees.

Dying to self is not an action in and of itself. It is a natural by-product of all the work that I am doing in you. Crucifying the flesh is simply you, with Us, agreeing with the sacrifice of Jesus. For Us it is: "Jesus died, so you also are dead." For you it is: "Jesus died as me, therefore, I am dead." The Son rose to new life so that Our people may do likewise. When He was raised, so were you, My Love. As He is, so are you, in this world.

As one who was raised from the dead and is now alive, you may stand before Us confident in the grace that empowers you to live and walk in truth. When opportunity for sin comes knocking, you can cheerfully present yourself to Us as one who is alive together with Christ. The truth will set you free. In Jesus, you are learning to be attracted to righteousness in the same way the Son experienced when He lived on Earth. There is a learned joy in obedience. The gift of grace with righteousness creates in you an attachment to Our Presence greater than any opposite lifestyle.

THE HOLY SPIRIT MAKES YOU HOLY

In the old man, you are always sin-conscious and therefore vulnerable to temptation. The new man, learning the holiness of Christ within, develops the same predetermined response to temptation that Jesus displayed on Earth. You do not wait for temptation to visit before making your declaration of righteousness. Like Jesus, you state, "It is written…" As one freed from sin and developing a passionate engagement with Me, you will have a guaranteed outcome of a sanctified lifestyle. In the gap between the temptation and the response is where sanctification is worked out between you and the wonderful Holy Spirit. His joy is a huge part of your partnership when the world, the flesh, and the devil try to usurp your new nature in Christ.

As you walk in the Spirit, you will not give in to the flesh. If you try to resist the flesh *without* being engaged with the Holy Spirit, you will struggle. As you abide in Our fellowship, it is our life together that will elevate your response and upgrade your lifestyle. This is an important point here, Beloved. It is the *Holy Spirit* in you who makes you holy. Walk with Him in partnership and the desires of the flesh will gradually and naturally get smaller by obedience to truth.

The good news is that the Spirit is absolutely in opposition against the flesh. When you are led by Him, it is His character and nature that will dominate your lifestyle. His love for you, joy in you, and peace over you are *immense*. His patience with your learning, kindness in your development, and goodness in the way He sees you are incredibly vast. His faithfulness to your life journey and gentleness with your mistakes will empower you to engage the self-control that it takes to deny the flesh any opportunity. Faithfulness, gentleness, self-control—nothing can ever work against the fruit of the Spirit.

WONDERFULLY LOVED FOREVER

It is your belonging to Christ that empowers you to stay dead to sin and remain alive to the Spirit. The truth that sets you free is that in Our heart you are both the subject and the object of Our love. We put Christ into you so that you would be subject to the same love that We have for One Another in the Godhead. Being set in Christ means you are loved in the same way as Jesus is loved. It is the same love that existed before the creation of all things. I love Myself in you.

When We put you into Christ, you became the object of Our love in Him. First love guarantees all love! You may love Us because We first loved you. Being in Christ means that you also may love as He loves. You may have the same passion, desire, and power to love that are within Jesus and allow that to govern all your other relationships. This means, God and humanity in the same space, doing the same things, in the same way. As He is, so are you in this world. When you are both the subject and the object of love, there is a double portion of favor available in all other relationships as well.

ALL VICTORY HAS A PAST TENSE

In the present, your life decisions are governed by a past victory. Your freedom is so great, you can practice being alive to Me, which means the by-product will be that you die daily. I give you permission to consider yourself to be dead. Your language here is past tense. Those who belong to Me *have been crucified* with me. Dying to self is simply the power of agreement with how We see you.

In that context, Beloved, dying to self should be an immense pleasure. Why? Because dying to self is not the focus. Practicing being alive to Me is where the fun is! There is a joy here that is so profound it will elevate your relationship with Me. It is the same glorious joy that elevated Jesus out of the grave that now elevates you into Our Presence. This joy is *loud,* Beloved. It is outrageous in its laughter, gladness, and rejoicing. Our pleasure in you marks you out for joy and laughter. You may count everything as joy because in Jesus you are marked by celebration!

As you practice being alive to Me, I want you to have an absolutely brilliant time. May your life be marked by wonder and astonishment at who you are becoming in Jesus. He endured the cross because the specific joy set before Him was *you*—living in the life, love, and laughter of Heaven here on Earth.

These things are written down for you so that Our joy may be in you and that your joy may always be full. There is only one way to grow up into all things in Jesus. It starts with a smile, develops into a grin, and becomes the infectious laughter of Heaven. Enter into the joy of the Lord!

DEEPENING MY RESPONSES TO LETTER 5

"We want you to live in the same quality of love that exists between Me, the Father, and the Holy Spirit. In that context, We want you to love your learning and welcome your growth opportunities. Then you can change enough to embrace the *next* thing We want to do for you, in you, and through you."

1. If you fully lived in the same quality of love that exists between Us, what would life look like for you? I'd love to hear your description.

2. When there is a "growth opportunity," how would you like to respond?

"Identity is the key to transformation... You do not become a new person by changing your behavior. You discover the person that you *already are* in Jesus and act accordingly."

1. What old-man habits and mindsets does this key lock up?

2. What new-man hopes and encouragement does it unlock?

3. When you envision yourself in Me, who do you see yourself to be?

4. How would you think, speak, and act?

"The new man in Christ is always making an agreement with the life within."

1. What would your new man like to agree with Me about?

2. Imagine us walking through this part of your new life. My life, righteousness, holiness, grace, faith, character, and power are all here for you. What am I doing? How do you respond to Me? I'd love to hear!

"Being alive to Me means that My way of living life becomes the truth of how you practice My Presence. Enjoy Our Presence as a reality in all your life circumstances."

1. Who would you like Me to be for you today? Make some notes.

2. Let's look at your day together. Which circumstances offer us some "Presence practice"?

3. At the end of the day, let Me know what was the most enjoyable part of our practice. Don't forget to ask Me what My favorite part was, too!

"Grace is Our empowering Presence that enables you to become the person that We see in Christ. We have a huge and boundless expectation towards you that is designed to fill you with all Our joy and peace in believing. This creates the same amazing expectation in you by the power of the Holy Spirit."

1. Think of a current situation where you want to encounter My empowering grace. Who am I excitedly expecting *you* to become through this adventure?

2. What is the empowering Presence I'm sharing with you?

3. How do you anticipate being more like Me when we're finished?

"As you focus on Our reciprocal joy, you will count all your circumstances as joyful even when they are difficult... Today you have Our blessing and permission to seize the new things that belong to you in Jesus."

Let's make a list of some of the circumstances in your life that We're joyful about. For each one listed, make a note of:

1. How are We using each situation as Our divine classroom?

2. What new things do you plan on seizing that belong to you in Jesus?

3. What makes Us smile as We watch you?

"As your mind becomes focused on the way that the Holy Spirit works in your life, a peace will overwhelm you. Peace is key to your development simply because learning is more difficult when you allow anxiety and stress to be present."

1. Where would you like My peace to overwhelm you?

2. What current limitations does that peace wash away?

3. Imagine a stress-free learning experience with Me. Describe it.

"In the gap between the temptation and the response is where sanctification is worked out between you and the wonderful Holy Spirit."

1. What is the righteousness you see in Me that you long to see in yourself?

2. Let's write some powerful declarations of those gifts of righteousness. "In You, I am and am becoming..."

3. What predetermined responses to temptation can we create together to empower you? "Because of Your… (love, kindness, etc.), I choose… instead of…"

"[The Holy Spirit's] faithfulness to your life journey and gentleness with your mistakes will empower you to engage the self-control that it takes to deny the flesh any opportunity. Faithfulness, gentleness, self-control—nothing can ever work against the fruit of the Spirit."

1. What hope does this truth give you?

"Dying to self is simply the power of agreement with how We see you."

1. What old mindsets about "death to self" does this truth lock away forever?

2. What new freedom does it unlock?

3. What would you like to agree with Us about as we go forward?

INVITATION TO RESPOND
Share Our Story

"Mature spirituality is an invitation to share, intermingle, and merge your personal story with Ours."

Imagine this entire letter as an invitation to share Our story. What's your response to Our invitation? What do you see Us inviting you into? What are you excited about discovering? What do you think is the next chapter of our story together? We can't wait to hear!

LETTER 6

Making War on Your Personal Negativity

KEY SCRIPTURES:

Exodus 3:14; Isaiah 9:6, 61:1-7; Matthew 11:27-30;

John 1:1-18, 8:12, 8:36, 14:27, 16:33; 1 Corinthians 13:12, 15:48-49;

2 Corinthians 3:8, 4:4-6; Galatians 2:20-21; Ephesians 1:3-23, 2:19-22;

Colossians 1:15-23, 2:13-14, 3:3, 3:9-10; Hebrews 1:3; James 1:23-25

Beloved,

If you are to rise up in My Son and take your place in the King-dom, it is essential that you see yourself as I see you. I put you in Him so that His Image may be seen in you and that you would constantly align with Our perspective, mindset, and language re-garding your identity.

JESUS IS YOUR MIRROR IMAGE

Jesus is the exact representation of God and you are being made into the glory of that image. Because your old man is dead and you are released to walk in newness of spirit, you have a divine advantage that We insist that you use in all your life situations. It is the gift of Presence. You are a habitation, Our dwelling place. We live in you and will never leave you alone.

Father, Son and Holy Spirit. The three in one! Each of Us is a mirror of the Other. We are different yet majestically reflect Each Other beautifully. You are enveloped by the Christ. We cannot look at you without seeing Him. This means that He is your mirror image! All things were created through Jesus and were made for Him. All things hold together in Him—including your life. Your life in the Kingdom only works powerfully when you see yourself in Him. He is in authority over everything: therefore, your life is marked by the same powerful perspective and language that We use when We talk about you.

In Him, you are wonderfully reconciled to the point where there is no stigma attached to you as you grow up in all things in Him. He who the Son sets free is absolutely free! It is God's good pleasure for all of Our fullness to dwell in Him. What does that mean for you? If Christ is in you, it means the same for you. In the Kingdom, the culture of the world has no substance. How you grew up on this Earth in your old fleshly ways has absolutely no relevance to how you grow up in Christ. In the Kingdom the way that you see, think, and speak must now reflect Him even as He reflected Me when He was a young child in the temple, a young man doing His blue-collar job, and as a mature man preaching the Kingdom with all the signs and wonders of that realm.

You are being presented in Jesus as holy, blameless, and beyond reproach. Living in Him has put your life on a higher place where everything is different. As you constantly put on the new self, the Holy Spirit will make sure that you will always be renewed to a true knowledge by experience, according to the image of the One.

I love your life! You will love it, too, when you see it from My viewpoint. I AM who I AM for you. I put you in Christ so that all that He is and all that He has, would also be yours. He is My mirror image and yours as well. He came to Earth to do My will, to reveal Us, and to make Us known in a new and living way. Everything Jesus said and did was a declaration of My nature and character. He knows Me the best of all creation and so do those to whom He reveals Me.

CHRIST WILL ALWAYS ACT WITHIN YOUR NEW MAN

Empowered by Me, Jesus came to speak Good News, to release captives, to open blind eyes, to free the downtrodden, and to proclaim favor over humanity. All these things He will do from His seat of authority in your heart and life from this day forward. As you partner with the kind intentions of My will for you, I will teach you how to abide in the full truth of who you are in Him.

Christ within is the new man with whom you are partnering for maturity. Christ is the mirror of what you look like in the spirit. It is My glorious life that I am giving to you. As you look into the mirror image of Jesus, you are being transformed into the same reflection. That same glorious light cuts through all the darkness to give your heart revelation of who you really are now and how you may grow up into the same powerful light. You are the light of the world, Beloved, as you learn to bear the same image as the One who adores you.

As Jesus is, so are you in this world. We all live face to face and eye to eye within the Trinity. This gives Him a defined perspective, also available to you since you sit with Him in heavenly places. This perspective easily sees how to overcome all obstacles. Having Him in your life is a decisive advantage for you in *every* possible way. You cannot ever be stopped, My child, except by your own mindset. He lives in your heart, giving you access to all-inclusive wisdom that allows you to live this life from the place We have chosen for the circumstances that swirl around you.

You have a rightful place of wisdom and power set aside for you in the Kingdom. It's yours and will never be taken away. However, you can miss out if you are not living from the right place. If you live from the world and not from the Kingdom, everything will be dimmer and more undefined. You will see through a mirror darkly when your own image is the only thing you can see reflected back at you.

The lens of your own history, the world you inhabit, and the relationships that have wounded you are all powerful opponents that can incapacitate your trust and faith. When you look through wrong, imperfect mirrors, you behold your old self. These broken images are not the new man in Christ. They have no clear image of Him, nor do they reflect the Kingdom of which you are a citizen.

THERE IS ALWAYS A KINGDOM PERSPECTIVE

The eyes through which you have been negatively viewed in the past are not the perspective that We have of you in the present as you move towards the future. The viewpoints of your family, school mates, work colleagues, and significant others all went to the cross in the old man. Indeed, every single negative decree from your past was taken out of the way. Every hostile, angry judgment was nailed to the cross.

When you see through the mirror of your past, it is your vision of your true self in Christ that is impaired and obscured. Similarly, when you see yourself only based on your performance and behavior, in any role or category, it is your acceptance in the Beloved that is undermined. Your old mirror will only keep you chained to shame, guilt, fear, and all the negative perceptions, mindsets, language, and emotions that they provoke.

Performance Christianity is the essence of bad news. The notion that who you really are is the result of your own performance is anathema to Me. The idea that I will only provide resources to those who perform well is *not* a new covenant truth.

I call you up to become a doer of My Word. One who hears but does not practice My Word is deluded, to be sure. In that context, you can only look in the natural mirror of a worldly perspective. You only see your old self, and you forget who you really are in Christ. In the Kingdom mirror, where you see your new man in Christ, you can be set free by the perfect law of liberty, which is this: "My old self has been crucified with Christ. It is no longer I who lives, but rather Christ who lives in me. So the life that I now live in my body, I live by trusting in the Son of God, who loves me and gave Himself for me."

So now there is no need to make My grace null and void. Accept who you are in the Kingdom, look through the mirror of Christ in you, and see yourself in Him—alive and spectacular! If you choose otherwise, you will lose connection with your own identity and revert back to negative thinking and emotions.

I do not want you to ever forget who you really are in Me. Do not lose touch with who you are becoming through the Spirit's powerful workings. People who hear but don't follow through can only forget the truth that creates freedom. When you abide in the truth, blessing is always the end result.

Just as you can carry the earthly image of your parents in looks, speech, and behavior, so too can you also bear My image. When your heart is fully engaged with Mine, there is a light that shines in you. It is the glory of the Spirit's indwelling Presence that brings a transformational reality. That same glory is the image of the One you adore. A lesser image brings a dullness of faith and blessing, because the mind has become blinded to the shocking brightness of Heaven's reality.

DOUBLE PORTIONS FREELY AVAILABLE

The key to personal breakthrough is always the death and resurrected life of Christ within. I love the truth that you are dead and your life is hidden with Christ in God. It sums everything up so perfectly. Jesus dealt with the old and I deal with the new, true you in Christ.

In Jesus, a double portion is set aside as a blessing to empower you to escape shame and humiliation. It's the perfect way to practice favor for yourself and vengeance on the enemy. As you apply this significant blessing, your shout of joy will release you to experience freedom. Fullness and abundance in the new covenant are reserved for the new-man lifestyle.

We intend to fully compensate you for all the violations inflicted on you from the world, the flesh, and the devil. The key concept We use in this context is the word "instead." It signifies an alternative. When a negative is present, We have other options for you in place of them.

There are so many promises that We have granted to you already. When a negative comes along, it is your opportunity to take Our relationship with you for granted! When something is already granted, there is no further request necessary. You take Me at My word and give thanks that you have already acquired something by promise and provision.

A promise may take a little time to come through, but you can live your life by it in the process. All delays are mostly about trust and trusting. Did We promise it to you? Then receive the joy and peace in believing. Promises are the currency of the Kingdom. They negate your circumstances and empower you to receive. They naturally impact your language.

The proclamations of God combine with the confessions of man to create a language that overcomes all obstacles. In this way, all the variables of life lead you to encounter Us and experience the goodness that produces your identity in fullness. I am your inheritance. As you live in Me, My life provokes blessing, favor, power, fullness, and overcoming in *your* life. Your life is the same as Mine!

How does this work? What belongs to Me and you? Beauty instead of ashes. The oil of joy instead of mourning. The garment of praise instead of heaviness. Instead of shame, a double blessing. Instead of dishonor and humiliation, a double portion. It's always double the recompense for what you have suffered.

EXPERIENCE DIVINE DISPLACEMENT

"Instead" means that We intend for the opposite to occur. Instead of being overpowered by what you are not, you can be overwhelmed by who Jesus is for you. It is your birthright to move in the opposite spirit. In this way, you are not consumed by a negative but rather learning to be overjoyed by the opposite.

I will use every negative to demonstrate to you the opposite, but you must be diligent to partner with Me in the process. This is called divine displacement. You will prosper from the alternative that I am releasing. Whatever negative confronts you, think the opposite, move towards it, and reposition yourself for a blessing. The ultimate favor is that every negative you think and feel is now designed to upgrade you and make you more in Our image.

Beloved, whatever negative thoughts you hold in your heart about yourself neutralizes your blessing in that area. When you agree with a negative, you will feel its bad effects. But when you confess who you are in Christ, His nature rises up within you and the truth sets you free. As you partner with what We say, you can receive the gift that is yours already in Him.

There is nothing negative in Christ; therefore, your mirror image in Him is the opposite of what you think and feel in your circumstances. There is no justification for a negative mindset or emotion in Christ. For example: In the normal pressure of life there are tensions and strains. Failure to deal with them from the right perspective causes a negative build-up of emotions leading to stress. Your confession could easily become, "I am so stressed out."

Our reality is that there is no stress in the Kingdom. Stress is caused by allowing pressure to produce a heavy load that becomes an emotional burden. Sleep flees, irritations become bigger, and you wear weariness like a coat. Stress is the absence of rest in your relationship with Jesus. You cannot get rid of a negative by confronting it! What you focus on, you empower.

Instead, you need to turn to Us. Jesus is your rest. He says, "Come to Me everyone who is weary and carries heavy burdens, and I will give you rest. Take My yoke upon you and let Me teach you. For I am gentle and humble in heart, and you shall find rest for your soul—your mind, emotions, and will. After all, My yoke is easy to bear and the burden I give you is light."

The proper response is for you to confess and partner with rest. Focus increases power. Do not deal with the negative. I have already done that for you on the cross. You cannot remove stress; rest will do that for you. As you partner with Me, you receive the gift of rest that is always resident within Me. Rest is not an antidote; it is a replacement emotion. Simply practice a constant thanksgiving that I am your rest. Do not try to feel restful or less stressed. Focus on Me and My rest as an act of celebration. It is not difficult, Beloved, and easier than you can imagine. Make war on your negativity all day and everyday by using this practice of Presence.

When you are anxious, it's the same process to learn. Anxiety is an absence of peace. Jesus can become your Prince of Peace. He said, "I leave My peace with you. It is not something the world can give, but I freely give it to you. Don't let your heart be troubled and don't let it be afraid." The world creates coping mechanisms to enable you to handle anxiety, but We want you to handle peace instead. It's Our gift to you! Do not try to remove anxiety; peace will do that for you.

If you know deeply that He is your Prince of Peace, your words will naturally confess it. It is His life—His peace—in you. You are not trying to appropriate peace by your own efforts but rather you can simply recognize that peace is who He is and He makes the gift of Himself available. Peace is not an antidote to anxiety; it's a replacement lifestyle that you practice by thanksgiving.

In the same way, We turn sorrow into joy. Worry flips over into confidence. Fear changes into courage. Rage is swallowed up by patience. Loss attracts redemption. Irritation releases delight. Neglect becomes appreciation. Disapproval invites honor. Resentment produces courtesy. Harshness becomes gentleness. Discouragement provokes favor. Meanness transforms into generosity. Anger releases contentment. Frustration becomes encouragement. Unfriendliness changes to kindness. What is hostile becomes amicable. Confusion attracts calmness. Agitation develops composure. The exhausted become refreshed. An offense can release a blessing. We simply love divine displacement. We hope you will too!

Beloved, in the world you will have tribulation, but be of good cheer because I have overcome the world! We have arranged for the negative things of the world around you to be replaced by an opposite found within the Kingdom. You are never disadvantaged even in times of persecution and suffering. Hold on to the life you know you have full access to—a place in Us where We are able to do exceedingly abundantly above all that you can ask or think.

When you are confronted by something negative, start by asking Me for the opposite word or blessing. I love this lifestyle! When you say, "I'm stressed," your body feels it immediately and your emotions tense up. When you say, "I have peace," everything relaxes. All negative perceptions, thoughts, and language create pressure points in your mind, emotions, and body that debilitate you because they act in line with your external circumstances.

Your new man in Christ lives from the inside to the outside. Therefore, My internal Presence is the starting place from where you begin your response to life situations. You are My habitation. You can connect with the peace that is already in you instead of engaging the anxiety around your life events. Christ in you and you in Christ—this is the best way to break negativity in your life. This is what it means to practice Presence.

It is My delight to make war joyfully on all your negatives. Whose side are you on? But have no worries. I will help you every step of the way. It's My pleasure to make you like Us.

DEEPENING MY RESPONSES TO LETTER 6

"Your life in the Kingdom only works powerfully when you see yourself in Jesus."

1. Tell Me about your current experience of Kingdom life. Write a general description.

2. What is working really well in our relationship?

3. Where are you feeling gloriously stretched?

4. When you look at yourself, where do you see Me reflected?

"It is My good pleasure for all of Our fullness to dwell in Him."

1. What does that mean for you? Share the implications for your everyday life.

2. Remember, there are not only implications for you but for Me too! What are the implications of this truth for Me?

3. How is this perspective different than your earthly experiences growing up?

4. What would you like to exchange from your past for My higher ways today?

5. What measured mindsets would you like to let go of?

6. What would you like to receive from Me instead?

"Living in Him has put your life on a higher place where everything is different... I love your life! You will love it, too, when you see it from My viewpoint."

1. Let's revisit the image of your life as a 100-story building. Consider what "floor" you are living on now in your experience of Me. (It may have changed since Letter #4!)

2. Think of a circumstance or an area of personal development that appears to be a large obstacle. Describe it briefly.

3. Now imagine My elevator of grace opening on your current floor. Push the button that says "Christ in you" and zoom up to My penthouse view. How does that same obstacle look now? Share your observations.

4. Also notice that you've walked into Our party celebrating you! What are we celebrating?

"As you look into the mirror image of Jesus, you are being transformed into the same reflection."

Becoming like Me is the result of beholding Me in worship, thanksgiving, prayer, Scripture, and encounters with Me as the living Word.

1. What previous life experiences have clouded your reflection of Me?

2. What are you beholding in Me that is transforming your perceptions and thinking?

3. When you look at My image, what do you see of yourself?

"Behold, every single negative decree from your past was taken out of the way. Every hostile, angry judgment was nailed to the cross."

1. What were the negative decrees made against you in your life by family, friends, teachers, employers, or anyone who should have cared for you?

2. See Me sitting peacefully with you as you take out a pen and paper. Make a list of the lies that were declared as truth about who you were.

3. Now you have a choice. You can hold on to your list and believe it to be true, or you can hand it to its rightful owner. That would be Me. I paid the price for everything on that list. It belongs to Me, not you. It's no longer your stuff. It's Mine. Beloved, give Me back My stuff! Now, let Me share with you My decrees of who you are. What are My opposites for every negative decree? Write them down.

4. None of My beloved ones has a right to live wounded. In Me, you have the right to be healed. This new list is your new

proclamation. Read My decrees of life aloud daily as an act of war on negativity.

5. After a month, consider how your image of yourself has transformed. Write a testimony about what is different.

And… no more taking back My stuff! Okay?

"Performance Christianity is the essence of bad news…. The idea that I will only provide resources to those who perform well is not a new covenant truth. I call you up to become a doer of My word."

1. How is performing for My acceptance different than being a doer of My word?

2. There are always two battles over your internal territory. One to take that *new man* territory and one to hold it. How does being a doer of My word help you hold the territory you've taken?

3. What are some enjoyable ways that you plan to follow through the breakthroughs you're receiving in My letters?

"In Jesus, a double portion is set aside as a blessing to empower you to escape shame and humiliation."

1. What are the exchanges of old for new life that I have for you? Write down a few of them.

2. What would a single portion of each look like?

3. What would a double portion look like?

4. What does each allow you to escape?

5. Describe the new possibilities that your double portion opens up for you!

"When something is already granted, there is no further request necessary. You take Me at My word and give thanks that you have already acquired something by promise and provision."

1. What are you still asking for that I've already promised you?

2. What current delays are you discovering to be opportunities to actively trust Me? What have I promised you for each one?

3. Create a Crafted Prayer that upgrades your language from asking "God, please…" to "Thank You that You promised…"[1]

4. Pray it with Me daily.

5. Take notes on what begins to transform in your confidence and joy.

"I will use every negative to demonstrate to you the opposite, but you must be diligent to partner with Me in the process. This is called divine displacement."

1. On one side of a paper, make a vertical list of the negatives in your behavior.

2. What is the opposite of each behavior in My true nature? Make a list of these for each of your negatives on the other side of your paper.

3. Tear the paper in half from top to bottom. Keep only the side of My opposites. At the top, write, "Through abundant grace and the gift of righteousness in Christ, this is who I am and am becoming."

---

1. See my book *Crafted Prayer* for more details on this type of prayer. Available at *www.BrilliantBookHouse.com.*

4. Read it aloud daily. Rejoice with Me as I rejoice over you.

5. Write to Me about what you discover!

"Our reality is that there is no stress in the Kingdom. Stress is caused by allowing pressure to produce a heavy load that becomes an emotional burden... Stress is the absence of rest in your relationship with Jesus."

1. Where would you like to exchange stress for rest in Me?

2. What promises do I have for you in those places? Write them out.

3. What am I celebrating in you right now?

4. What are you celebrating in Me?

5. Imagine Me knocking on the "door" to a stressful situation.

   a. Are you willing to open it to Me?

   b. Do you want Me to come in as your Prince of Peace?

   c. What is the look on My face? What is the tone of My voice?

   d. What will we talk about that renews our relationship of rest and trust?

"It is My delight to make war joyfully on all your negatives. Whose side are you on?"

1. Imagine us sitting in a war room, looking at a map of your life. Who is currently winning the war on negativity?

2. Whose side have you been on?

3. Whose side are you on now? Let's plot our plan for advancement!

4. What internal territory do you want Me to invade and overwhelm?

5. Describe the current threats to that territory.

6. Who will I be for you in each of these?

7. What do I have in My arsenal of promises for our invasion? Let's make a list.

8. How will you partner with Me in this offensive against the enemy of your soul?

INVITATION TO RESPOND

Thanksgiving of Rest

"Simply practice a constant thanksgiving that I am your rest."

Write a thank-you note to My Son for who He is as your rest and peace. Fill it with your discoveries, joys, and delights in what He means to you as your Prince of Peace.

LETTER 7

Unclaimed Upgrades, Part 1:
The Foundations of Upgrades

KEY SCRIPTURES:

Genesis 1:26; Isaiah 42:8; Jeremiah 29:11-13; Malachi 3:6;

Matthew 6:33, 7:7; Luke 18:1-8; John 3:27, 4:1-29, 5:7-21, 10:7-9,

14:6, 14:13-14, 15:4-15, 17:1-23; Romans 6:4, 7:6, 8:31-39, 11:35-36;

1 Corinthians 2:12; 2 Corinthians 1:19-20, 5:17; Ephesians 1:3-6;

Colossians 13:1-4; 2 Timothy 1:12; Hebrews 13:5-8

Beloved,

Since the beginning I have wanted a people for Myself, a people
for whom I would be their God and whom I would elevate into
a high place in My affections. A people who, in the midst of their
circumstances, could taste My goodness, thrive, and prosper. That
is the salvation story. The freedom to live in Me in all the joy and
peace in believing. To be loved by Us in the same way that We
love One Another. A people who could be confident in Our
unchanging nature.

GOD'S INTENTION BECOMES MAN'S PURPOSE

I create your experience in the light so that you can love being in the light with Me and learn how to walk as a free person made whole. You are part of My story in primary purpose. I am part of your journey to become like Me. We are inseparable on this journey. We have made all the provisions and resources you will ever need for this unfolding journey.

My intention and joy is to initiate everything you require. Your purpose and joy is to respond to Me in every life situation. In this way, you grow up in Christ in all things. There is always a gift being given. Jesus said, "My Father works and I work. I only do what the Father is doing. I only say what He is saying." He responded perfectly to what I was creating around and through Him.

I am making all things new in your life; therefore, you are learning how to do all things in a new way also. I am not rehashing the old. I am not salvaging parts of the old and reusing them in your new man. I have given you newness of life so that you may serve Me in newness of spirit. Because you are a new creation, you must learn to see, think, speak, walk, and act differently from the world around you. You are *in* the world but not *of* it. You belong to the Kingdom. You live in a realm vastly superior in every way. What you have learned in the world will not serve you in the Kingdom.

Beloved, upgrades come down into your life from Heaven to lift you into a higher state of being in Christ. They elevate you to the same level of expectation that Jesus enjoyed on Earth. I love to initiate new things in you, for you, to you, and around you. Expectation always asks for favor. You have not because you don't ask. We are together in all things, partners in expectation.

My wisdom elevates you above worldly knowledge. It is the understanding of how I see, think, speak, and act. I lead; you follow. I initiate; you respond. What I start will release a gift as you respond to Me. That initial step always determines the condition for what is to follow. Example: The death of the old man is a gift from Me, courtesy of Jesus. You took no part in that act. Death to self is a gift that began in the Kingdom and is made real by the Holy Spirit on Earth. You received a radical permission to now consider yourself dead and to be alive to God. The gift of death sets you up to receive the gift of life. That's an amazing upgrade: new for old.

When I initiate and you respond, you are delivered from the virus of religious performance. This is you trying to touch and connect with Me by your own efforts. As Jesus is, so are you in this world. He lived in the same reality that you must now embrace. Everything the disciples received from Jesus was given to Him by Me. Jesus never acted on His own initiative. I initiated; He responded. Jesus' actions did not come before My initiative. This is true for you as well. Everything I give to you out of love invites a response from you. You can do nothing to enter this life. Salvation is a gift. You must do everything to stay in this life. That is abiding: living connected to Me in the same way Jesus did.

Initiating and responding are the precedents that I set in My beloved Son so that you would follow the same pattern of living from your identity in Me. You are buried with Him in baptism and raised up to walk in newness of life by the action of My glory. In this new elevation, you can set your mind on things above, because you are dead to all things below. A religious system focused on behavior is not designed to create freedom. Only your identity in Christ and His identity embedded in you can empower you to relate to My nature as a way of life to be fully enjoyed. In Christ, you have My DNA as part of your ongoing life experience. The ultimate permission is that in Jesus you have the DNA to receive fullness!

OUR NATURE IS THE FOUNDATION OF TRUST

You change when you see My unchanging heart. I do not change, Beloved. Every great gift you receive comes from the One with whom there is nothing deceitful, two-faced, or fickle. The unchanging heart and the unchanging Word become the places where you can stand in absolute confidence. My goodness will not cease towards you, regardless of circumstances or your place in them. I am teaching you to respond to your identity in Christ, not your circumstances. There you can feel totally secure in His DNA in you as you process the situation in wisdom and trust. When life is unstable, Jesus is the only constant. His nature is foundational for all your life responses.

It is impossible for Me to see you disconnected from love. You are accepted in Me so that you can learn how to abide in Me using My nature. If you refuse to embrace My nature, turn away from the fruit of the Spirit as your lifestyle, and reject emotional attachment to Me, then you will face a long hard road. I will not leave you nor forsake you if you do not want to practice life in Christ, but My Presence will not carry the reality that I want for you. You will find the power of salvation when you constantly turn towards Me in the joy and peace of believing.

The goal of the Holy Spirit is to produce a strong conviction in your heart regarding My faithfulness towards you, a firmly held belief in who I am for you. I want you to learn to believe implicitly and have a full assurance of understanding. All the great men and women of God had a certainty of and a reliance on My integrity towards them.

You cannot cling to a perception of yourself that partners with the flesh. You cannot become a saint if you see yourself as a sinner. When you see yourself in Christ, His mind in you causes you to think like a saint and the sinner focus automatically starts to die out in you. It is replaced with the thinking from above, which is the mind focused on the Spirit, not the flesh. In this way, you are developing convictions that connect you to all that I am for you.

We would like you to get out of the mindset that your humanity is greater than Our majesty. People think that "being real" is to acknowledge fear, doubt, anxiety, and stress when it is present. How can you acknowledge something that has already been killed off on the cross? I'm not asking you to deny the existence of the negative. I'm requesting that you don't make it so real that your old nature is running the show. The new man has direct access to all the fruit of the Spirit, which is the most "real" you can experience in a stressful moment. The new man can always take you higher in Me. This is the place where what you see, think, and say about how you face life in the world is being upgraded by the new man. In this context "being real" stems directly from Me being your habitation. "Being real" is you practicing abiding in Me.

You were chosen to receive the unconditional, ever-present love that flows between the Father and the Spirit and Me. You are bound together with Our joyful unity. You therefore can experience the same quality of passionate and relentless love. Life situations may not reduce, but their purpose is for you to increase! The world does not get smaller. It is you who enlarges to the point of being transformed. That's fullness! No matter what the world throws at you, the Kingdom compels you to grow up into all things in Me.

JESUS IS THE RECIPIENT OF YOUR PROVISION

Beloved, We know how tough things can be in the world. Life can be a crisis, a battleground, a minefield of relational difficulties to add to the ongoing stream of problems, betrayals, and day-to-day hardships. This is why We talk to you about living above, not beneath, the line of privilege in Christ. The reason We put you into Christ and put Him into you is so that you would always have power and Presence in every circumstance of life. Being in Christ is full-on relentlessly Good News. Every day this is spectacular news of great joy. We do not ever minimize the hard issues of life, and We ask in return that you trade them in for the joy and peace in believing who We are for you in Jesus. There is no sense in living from a problem-centered world when you can live in the possibility-focused Kingdom.

Israel had a choice to return to Egypt or continue on their journey to a land of promise. The space in between is about training. Part of that training is becoming acclimated to the atmosphere of the Kingdom. The roadway was altered with promises, instructions, and tough moments. Every need was met in spectacular fashion: heavenly food just waiting to be picked up; water gushing from a rock; breakfast flying in by air; a cloud protecting them by day and a pillar of fire by night.

Yet the people fantasized about vegetables and wanted to return to Egypt. The same people who cried out for deliverance wanted to return to the place of oppression because they thought it was better and safer than My Presence. Learning how the Kingdom works while on planet Earth is not easy, but it is a great lifestyle!

Your choices are simple: Stay as you are or become like Me. Conceptually that's not a difficult choice but that is where the fantasy ends. Practically, that choice means a number of big changes and a myriad of small adjustments. They do not all come at once but they *do* come and I will be there with you to meet every single test.

You must face everything from Our nature, which is your new personality in Christ. You cannot grow or live effectively if you face a world of difficulties with the old-man mindset, perspective, and language. My goal is not to teach you survival tactics in the world. It is to train, equip, and elevate you to live in the Kingdom;

to live in every way, from Heaven to Earth. I do not want you to try to live the best life possible in Egypt when Jesus—your land of promise—is totally available at all times. I don't want you to navigate this world. I am not training you to slalom your way around problems and hardships. You do not have to live in a dystopian world when the majesty of My Kingdom is available in and through Jesus.

The training is often about elevation. Think from above not below. Vision is not just about the direction you are going in; it's about the height in Jesus at which We want you to travel. It's learning a new language because you are in a very different country. It's about a way of seeing life that is totally breathtaking and beautiful. Along the way, truth and life will change your lens, renew your mind, and rob you of every piece of negativity. The Kingdom is a constant, relentless series of upgrades.

Upgrades come to you in dreams, through Scripture, from revelations in life, through encounters with Presence, from wisdom in mentoring, from prophecies and visions. They also come in problems, difficulties, grief, loss, battle, opposition, and persecution. Every hard, hateful word spoken against you can be upgraded to a promise because of the life within you. It is not possible to establish victory as a lifestyle if there are no battles to fight in life. You cannot learn the way of an overcomer if there is nothing to overcome!

Beloved, know deep inside your heart that We do not create problems for you to overcome. We simply use the situations, scenarios, and relational difficulties in a problem-focused world to train you in the way, the truth, and the life of the Kingdom. The best place to start is with your placement in Jesus and what that means in the Kingdom. I will love you in exactly the same way that I love Jesus. I will treat you in exactly the same way. As He is, so are you in this world. You are a joint heir with Him so that you can learn to receive all the resources of Heaven available in and through Him. You have His name on your lips so that you may receive just as He would in your life situations. And He has your name written on His hand.

In Christ, I have qualified you to receive. You are learning to ask in line with your "credit rating" in Jesus. Prayer is about learning to abide in what I have promised and asking in line with My will and desire for you. The best prayer always has a relational base and a functional outcome. In Christ, you are learning to pray with Me, not towards Me. Find your favorite place in Jesus to commune with Me. Let us talk confidentially together. I know everything anyway; I just like to hear you share with Me.

You are learning how to ask, seek, and knock in a way that causes you to move into what We have already determined for you to receive in Our Presence. You are in Christ and We have given you powerful promises that are connected to your identity. In Heaven that identity is true in the present and those promises empower you to grow into a powerful future, regardless of what is against you.

I am so excited for you to learn the "Yes and Amen" that is in My heart toward you. It's My passion for you that guarantees the outcome. As you partner with Me in becoming Christ-like, the outcome will always be a done deal in My heart. One of My favorite verses in the Scripture about you is Ephesians 2:10 (My paraphrase): "You are My workmanship, created in Christ Jesus for good works, which I have prepared beforehand for you to walk in, with Me!" I hope that image is as beautiful to you as it is for Me.

In any situation, ask for a promise or use one that you already know has power and life for you. Abide in the word of promise, power, and purpose. Pray from that place of confidence. Pray like one who is loved. Don't pray like a widow when you can pray like a bride! Enjoy praying to the One who knows you the best and loves you the most. All prayer is part of a love covenant between Me and the Father. When you pray from your identity and your promises, you announce your presence in Me: "This is who I am in Christ."

When you ask as I would ask and in My name, the Father will certainly do it so that the Father will be glorified in Me. Beloved, We will not give Our glory to another—but you are *not* another. You are in Me! You are filled with the Holy Spirit. You are My workmanship. You are My joint heir and therefore a full heir with Me. You are My Body. You are My Beloved. You are My Bride. You are My passion, My delight, and My desire. You are most definitely not just another! Did you hear that?!

Jesus is the recipient of your provision. It comes to you because you are in Him. He has already accepted what you need to receive. You are accepted in the Beloved. You are now practicing that acceptance in every circumstance of life. Jesus is the evidence of your provision. You are a joint heir with Him. Accept that and step into it. You have a credit rating in Heaven that is huge. In Christ you are prequalified to receive. The DNA to receive is already active in the new man in Jesus.

Agree to live in Christ and you will know His Presence. Agreement creates a different reality. It's a new exciting experience that needs constant repeating. Repetition is the key to becoming. Practice is the art of growing up in all things in Christ. Keep on asking, joyfully and relationally, because the DNA to receive is already within you. Why the repetition in prayer? It is to give you the opportunity to practice your identity in Jesus in prayer. You are learning to ask in a way that makes it possible for your spirit to say yes! How? By using the promises I gave you. If you abide in Our words, ask whatever you desire, and it will be done.

Start with the outcome and work backward. Start with what you need to receive. Start with the gift that I want to give you. Beloved, you focus on the outcome so that you can understand and enjoy the process. The outcome creates confidence in Me. The process produces the trust that leads to faith increasing within you. Find the promise that unlocks everything and ask in line with it.

Look for My Presence that is always present. How do you seek My Presence when I never leave you? You seek Me with anticipation and excitement. You look for Me knowing that I am right there in your situation. I love declaring My intentions towards you. I want you to use that intention as a calling card empowering you to connect with My heart. What you receive in Christ opens your heart to look for increase through repetition. Your testimony creates the opportunity to receive continually. Come looking for ultimate goodness. A life that adores the Kingdom will always love where it is displayed. Seek first the Kingdom lifestyle in Christ and He will be the Source for all that you need.

Seek in a way that makes you find! Set your mind on what I will to give you. Seek what you know is already yours. My permission is clear: you will find it! Look in a whole new way.

DEEPENING MY RESPONSE TO LETTER 7

"My intention and joy is to initiate everything you require. Your purpose and joy is to respond to Me in every life situation."

1. What did I just free you from with that statement?

2. What are you free to become more of?

3. What are you free to become less of?

"I am making all things new in your life; therefore, you are learning how to do all things in a new way also. I am not rehashing

the old... I have given you newness of life so that you may serve Me in newness of spirit."

Did you know that when you are doing something new, you can't make a mistake? You can only learn! Fear of a mistake is often why people return to old, familiar ways. So let's step up into the new together.

1. What new upgrades feel a bit awkward right now?

2. How does it help knowing that you are simply practicing something new?

3. Make a list of what you're learning so far. I'd love to hear!

4. What provision have I already made to help you convert "new things" to an upgraded life?

5. As you live more in My newness, the light will illuminate old ways you've tried to renovate. Identify what they are. What are my brand-new upgrades for each?

"Expectation always asks for favor. You have not because you don't ask. We are together in all things, partners in expectation."

Favor is My special preference towards you. It's My passion to promote you. It's My intentional bias towards you as my privileged and highly regarded one!

1. So what is the favor that you long to ask of Me?

2. Make Me a list of your requests—and be sure to ask with language that is full of expectation, thanksgiving, and joy, believing that I have already provided everything you require.

3. Now look around your life in the coming days and weeks. When you see My favor manifest towards you, make a note of it.

4. In a few weeks, you'll begin to see just how many gifts of favor I've had waiting! Keep a list. When a struggle presents itself, you can read the list again and it will trigger worship and help you refocus on your new man.

"As Jesus is, so are you in this world... I initiated; He responded. Jesus' actions did not come before My initiative. This is true for you as well. Everything I give to you out of love invites a response from you."

1. How is receiving a gift different than picking up a paycheck?

2. Where would you like to be delivered from the virus of religious performance?

3. What am I freely giving you in love?

4. What changes for you when I become the initiator and you become the responder?

"You change when you see My unchanging heart."

1. How would you complete this thought?

   b. "Father, when I see Your... I become..."

   c. "Jesus, when I see Your... I become..."

   d. "Holy Spirit, when I see Your... I become..."

2. Create as many of these sentences as you can. Read them aloud often.

3. What happens in your heart when you focus on Mine?

"All great men and women of God had a certainty of and a reliance on My integrity towards them."

Think of a "hero of the faith." It can be someone from the Bible, someone in history, or a believer you have known.

1. Tell Me why you chose this particular man or woman.

2. Describe their certainty in who I have been for them.

3. Write about their willing reliance on My integrity in their lives.

4. What do you identify with in their lives that would also describe your own?

"We would like you to get out of the mindset that your humanity is greater than Our majesty... I'm not asking you to deny the existence of the negative. I'm requesting that you don't make it so real that your old nature is running the show."

1. Beloved, where have you made your humanity greater than My majesty?

2. How could you acknowledge a negative without letting your old nature run the show? Give Me an example from your everyday life to go with your answer.

3. Describe how you plan to "be real" from here forward?

"The world does not get smaller. It is you who enlarges to the point of being transformed. That's fullness!"

1. How does that truth change the game for you?

2. How will you perceive your circumstances in a new way?

3. How will you think about the world differently?

4. What is the impact on your language from this truth?

"We do not ever minimize the hard issues of life, and We ask in return that you trade them in for the joy and peace in believing who We are for you in Jesus."

Tell Me about the hard situations for you. Then choose one for us to practice with.

1. Imagine each One of Us coming to you with a gift. Inside is who We will be for you in that issue. What have each of Us brought you?

2. See the situation on one side, then see the size of Our gifts on the other. Our gifts to you are wrapped in joy and peace. Your gift to Us is giving us your problem. Make as many trades as you want. Each one brings Us great joy!

"Beloved, know deep inside your heart that We do not create problems for you to overcome. We simply use the situations, scenarios, and relational difficulties in a problem-focused world to train you in the way, the truth, and the life of the Kingdom."

What are the situations in your life that are training you in My Kingdom realities?

For each of your challenges:

1. What are you learning about My higher ways?

2. Which truths are moving from concept to reality?

3. How is this situation making My ways and truth part of your everyday life?

4. What changes when you view your difficulties from My elevated perspective?

5. How are you being trained as an overcomer?

6. What upgrades are you experiencing and how did each one come to you?

"In Christ, you are learning to pray with Me, not towards Me."

The Son's full-time job now is praying for you (Romans 8:34). The Holy Spirit prays prayers so deeply felt, they don't have words (Romans 8:26).

Have you ever wondered what We are praying? And wouldn't you want to pray that, too?

1. Come rest with Me and listen. Rejoice, worship, and relax in My Presence. I'll initiate My prayers and promises for you. You can respond by praying and declaring them with Me.

2. Write down what we pray together. Find the promises that unlock everything and ask in line with those. Revel in praying with Us, as the beloved one you are.

3. Delight in being with Us until the answer manifests. We do! Enjoy practicing your identity in Jesus in prayer. Become stronger, more peaceful and confident while waiting with Me.

"Jesus is the recipient of your provision. It comes to you because you are in Him. He has already accepted what you need to receive. You are accepted in the Beloved. You are now practicing that acceptance in every circumstance of life."

1. What new freedom does this truth unlock for you?

2. What old performance mindsets does it lock up?

3. Where can you practice your acceptance today?

INVITATION TO RESPOND
Opening Your Upgrades

"Beloved, since the beginning I have wanted a people for Myself."

In that one line is the purpose for all of these letters! Think about it. You are My dream—and every upgrade you claim is a dream come true for Me.

I initiated you being with Me. I initiated this stockpile of upgrades for you to receive. Write and tell Me your response! What upgrades do you want to receive first? What are you excited to discover for each? How does it feel to know there are so many?!

LETTER 8

Unclaimed Upgrades, Part 2:
Learning the Upgraded Life

KEY SCRIPTURES:

Matthew 11:28-30; John 2:13-14, 4:1-26, 5:4-5, 10:1-10, 12:49-50,

14:8-17 & 27, 16:13-15; Romans 8:28, 12:2 & 21; 1 Corinthians 1:7, 15:57;

Ephesians 1:5 & 18-23, 3:20; Philippians 3:8-16; Colossians 3:2;

Philemon 6; Hebrews 4:14-16; 2 Peter 1:2-4; Revelation 3:7-8 & 20

Beloved,

Knowing that the gift of God is available to you is the key to your current life issues. It becomes the "stance" you take in your circum*stance*. To the Samaritan woman struggling with some hard life issues, He came with a message of freedom. If she knew the gift of God that was present for her, then life would become completely different. There is a gift waiting for you in all your life situations. Expectation in Christ means that you lack no gift.

RECOGNIZE WHAT BELONGS TO YOU IN JESUS

The spirit of the world cannot teach you the ways of the Kingdom. Receive My Spirit today so that your learning can be upgraded. Then you will know the things that I freely want to give you. The gift of the Holy Spirit is given so that you can know what is available to you in any situation. He will take what belongs to Me and will give it to you. Every circumstance requires revelation. The Spirit of Truth will lead you into encountering the plans, purposes, and possibilities that are at your disposal. You overcome by what you can receive from Me when you are under pressure. Don't you just love the very idea of that?

What is possible for you to receive from Me in your present situation? What is preventing you from accepting delivery? Are you listening properly? Did you pick up on My heart for you? Do you secretly believe that My word to you is a negative? Are you fearful, worried, anxious, or panicked? Do you feel angry, frustrated, or unbelieving? Sometimes, Beloved, your natural disposition is the blockage to receiving.

Why not receive My love right here? No shame, guilt, or condemnation—just love. Jesus accepted punishment in your place, so there is no penalization required. Why not receive My peace right here? It's a different kind of peace than the world can give. In the world, you are taught to work on anxiety, stop being fearful, and somehow learn not to worry—which of course does the opposite. Whatever you focus on you empower.

Kingdom peace is a pure gift of peace. When you receive peace, the action of stillness creates a calm, restful serenity that fills up your inner space and pushes out all negative emotions and thoughts.

Our gift to you is a stress-free life! Stress is a by-product of a life not focused on Christ within. The Prince of Peace must take up residence. He creates a new realm within you that overcomes the pressures of the external world. Your spirit within is always in the Presence of God, therefore always at rest. Your soul with its outward connection to the world is always vulnerable to pressures.

Your soul must come under the rule of the inner man of Christ where your spirit mingles with Ours in newness of life.

This is not a discipline to practice. A gift is not a discipline—it is a delight! If someone gives you a beautiful item of clothing, you do not discipline yourself to wear it. You delight in putting it on and displaying it to others. The peace We give you is just like that, a pure gift that, when you accept, will itself push out any negative. Let yourself feel My peace. Concentrate on being calm, still, and loving peace. What you focus on becomes your reality.

When you take Our yoke upon you, it becomes possible for you to experience a partnership with Us that is out of this world. You get to learn from Our attitude and approach to life by embracing Our nature and character as your own. Our yoke is much easier than the world and Our burdens are much lighter. The lack of real partnership makes life hard, sharp, pressured, and the burdens of life in all its forms can overwhelm your emotions. You become weary, heavy laden, needing to accept and practice rest.

Life in the Spirit is about learning to recognize what belongs to you already because Jesus lives in you. It is so important to acknowledge who Jesus is within your spirit. It's vital to admit to yourself what is *already* yours in Christ and to express gratitude and thanks for what He has done in you. Then you get to call it up in you when you are under pressure. My Presence is not separate from your life issues and trials. I am at the heart of everything you face. My nature is now your internal disposition. You are being trained to be made alive together with Christ, and to learn to live aware of Me and to practice being responsive to all that We are in you. Practice the lifestyle of being in Me.

That practice has two applications. Firstly, in the immediate situation you must gain control of the circumstances. How do you do that? Learn the lesson you need in order to stand calmly in Me.

111

Rehearse your responses. Do the same drill over and over. Exercise your trust and faith by confession and declaration. This is your life routine that becomes your spiritual rhythm that overcomes the natural pressures and problems. Keep repeating out loud the faith that is in your heart, love the learning, and take delight in who you are becoming.

Do not make those responses purely circumstantial. That is called situational spirituality where you only practice those responses until the issue subsides. The failure to *practice them until it becomes your lifestyle* means that you let go of the most important part of the upgrade. You favor the resolution of the problem more than growing in relationship with Me. When you put function before relationship, you become poor in spirit.

The second application is to upgrade what you have won into a new custom, habit, normal routine, and way of life. You build on this victory, pulling it into your relationship with Me so that subsequent problems and issues have a new starting place in Presence, trust, and faith. It becomes your usual experience, a pattern, a typical response for you to move *from* victory, not towards it. You live *from* the victories you have gained previously because they are your new normal. In this way, the consistent victories in Christ become an overcoming mentality and lifestyle in the Spirit. When you hit the level of overcoming in life, you are now living *above* your circumstances, not beneath. Set your mind on things above, not on things below on the earth.

The lifestyle of an overcomer produces the mentality of one who is more than a conqueror. It is a learned behavior that arises because of your identity in Christ. As I am, so are you in this world. Identity and behavior upgrade your perspective, mindset, and language to the point where transformation takes place. You become seasoned and accomplished in your walk with Me. It is the real mark of maturity and growth. Always allow yourself to be challenged upwards in your circumstances.

You are learning to press on towards the real goal of the upward call of God in Me. Our vision of you will always carry an upgrade. In every situation, We see something that will lift you up. When you set your mind on things above, you are learning how We see things so that you can arrange your thinking around Our perspective. The Holy Spirit works with you to synchronize your thoughts with Mine—the mind of Christ. Acknowledgement of who you are in Me is a key part of that joy-filled process.

KNOCK ON THE EVER-OPEN DOOR

I have opened a door for you in My Son that will be forever unlocked. It was important for the Kingdom to have Jesus describe Himself as the Door. The word We chose means a gateway, an imposing entrance. He is the portal to another dimension of life and reality. Anyone moving from a world perception to a Kingdom perspective must go through Him. That door has been open for more than two millennia.

In every situation you face, He is the door to all your possibilities. I have opened a door that no one can close. What is the door of opportunity that Jesus wants to be for you in your current situation? Do you need an entrance to employment, better health, wholeness, finances? Do you need an exit from a harmful, destructive lifestyle? Do you need a door into favor, permission, and blessing?

Right now I am knocking on the door of your opportunity, reminding you of My available Presence and grace for you. There is always new territory to explore in the Kingdom. When We open a new door to something higher and larger, We will talk to you about possibilities. As you enter this new space, We will immediately or eventually close the door behind you so that you cannot stay in a place that is familiar and comfortable. We agreed that I, the Comforter, would need to live inside of you because We have always intended to take you out of your comfort zone.

There are times when you can feel that a way forward in life is obstructed or restricted on one level. You feel frustrated, discouraged, and discontent. Sometimes you have to learn patience, perseverance, or determination so that you can practice endurance with joy. On other occasions, I want you to realize that the barrier in front of you is My way of saying that your time is over on this level. An upgrade is available and Jesus is knocking at the door of opportunity.

Let Me say again, Beloved, when the functionality (issues, problems, and difficulties) of life come against you, it is time to upgrade your relationship with Me first. If you don't take time to go deeper with Me, you will simply bring your list of things you want done—and nothing will happen. *Everything* I do is relational. That is why I ask you to rejoice always and give thanks constantly. It's not that I need the worship. It's *you* who needs to rejoice and be happy in Me for your soul's sake. I love worship because I get to engage with you. But worship is great for you because it refocuses your lens back onto Me and off the small-minded perspective your old man wants to focus on.

When you put relationship with Me as a priority in every life issue, your growth will be phenomenal. Never downsize My majesty, because then you will downgrade your trust, faith, and favor. That will lead you into avenues of fear, anxiety, worry, doubt, unbelief, low self-esteem, and condemnation. When you entertain any form of negativity, you make an agreement with redundancy.

My Presence empowers rejoicing, thanksgiving, and worship so that your trust and faith can rise up to receive. Presence releases the joint heir in you so that you can step into your inheritance.

Identity theft is the #1 crime in the world. Someone is stealing from you in the spirit! In Scripture We wrote down everything We want to do for you. If everything in Me is "Yes and Amen," how on Earth did you hear "No"? I have blessed you with every blessing in the heavenly places. That means you need to come up there in your spirit and renewed mind to receive it. That's what an upgrade looks like to Me. The Father has made claims on you by putting you in Me, the Beloved Son. The Father wants you to claim your blessing in My name! Your response is to agree with the Father's claim and position yourself to receive.

I'm not talking about you *on your own initiative* "naming and claiming," "grabbing and blabbing" something you want to have for yourself. We want you to agree with Our claim on you for this particular circumstance. That claim comes in the form of a promise, a specific favor, or the kind intention of Our will. The point is that *I initiate* the claim and I set the range and scope of your upgrade. I love upgrades! It is so exciting to watch you respond, develop, and grow into this new space that I open up for you in Jesus.

What if there are dozens, scores, or even hundreds of unclaimed upgrades in your life? When I make a claim on you, I am asserting a right, purchased by Jesus' blood, to promote, advance, and elevate My relationship with you in My Son. I want to raise your status. I want to replace old with new. When something is unclaimed by you, you may sense a loss. I certainly feel the loss of a deeper relationship with you; I hope you do, too. So let's get together!

The enemy is a claim jumper. Since he lost his relationship with Me, the hatred and vindictiveness he feels towards Me drives him to steal, kill, and destroy any relationship with My people. You'll know when this happens when you lose confidence in Me or he blinds you to the possibilities of what belongs to you in Jesus. The negativity that consumes him is what he wants *you* to receive.

Beloved, I am relentless in everything I do. My nature is relentless towards you, every moment, every hour, every day. If My love is not relentless towards you, it will fail you when you need it most. If My joy is not relentless towards you, it is impossible for you to count all things as joy. You are at your strongest when you constantly feel My joy, hear My laughter, and live each day under My smile. If My peace is not relentless towards you, then worry, anxiety, and panic will catch up to you. If I am not relentless in My goodness and kindness, you cannot repent and turn around in your circumstances. If grace does not abound towards you, then it will be difficult for you to have confidence in your High Priest Jesus, which means you may not experience the mercy and grace to help you when you need it most. I am consistent, persistent, unfaltering, unflagging, unrelenting, and unstoppable in My loving kindness and deep affection for you. I love you in the same way that I love Jesus.

Because We are relentless, I have appointed the Holy Spirit as your personal Claim Assessor. He guides you into all truth. He takes what belongs to Jesus and gives it to you. He trains you in understanding the claims of Heaven. He empowers you to respond and ask. He authorizes you to receive and enables you to live in that new space. He holds the license to Our claim on you and your claim on Jesus. He qualifies you to receive and commissions every upgrade.

Revelation elevates your awareness of who I am for you and therefore upgrades who you can become in Me. Part of that is you recognizing that your DNA in Jesus empowers you to partner with Me to create the reality that releases new life.

Knock on the door that is never closed to you. In your own life, when a door is open and you know that someone is present, you knock differently. You knock with expectation. You call out a greeting, anticipating an answer. You knock on an open door so that it swings open wider. That is expectation at work.

What is opening up for you at this time? Start knocking on the door with expectation of something opening up!

Also remember that I am knocking at your open door wanting greater access to your heart. I am looking for fellowship. What do I want to be for you next? Enjoy the asking and seeking. This next time period does not have to be a struggle; it can be a dance—not warfare, but a waltz.

You can count on My unchanging nature, My relentless consistency, and My pattern of predictability. That means you can include My constancy as part of your anticipation. It's much easier for you to learn patience if you take My dependability into account. I love it when you factor in My unchanging reliability to your circumstances. Together *we* are unbeatable.

In Christ you are also governed by the same law of the Spirit of Life that is in Him. So you are enjoying a relationship and partnership forged in love, peace, and joy. Situations confirm, firstly, that you are in Jesus by the way that you respond to Me. That's His image in you shining through. Secondly, situations determine your personal identity in Jesus by the way that you lean into Him in trust and faith.

MY PROMISES ARE ALWAYS BIGGER
THAN YOUR CIRCUMSTANCES

Beloved, you have My undivided attention and affection. My heart is always fully fixed on Jesus. When I include you in that same wonderful space, you become a partaker of the divine nature. I want you to establish this truth as a life value and principle that will never change. Grace and peace will always be multiplied to you in the life process of moving in both knowledge and experience of God and of Jesus your Lord.

As you practice focusing on who We are for you, all the qualities of Jesus become available by My divine power and excellence. I grant you unconditionally and specifically to receive everything connected to My life and godliness. I want you to have it *all.*

Every one of your life issues is thrilling to Me because I can create anything I want to upgrade your life. Some situations may contain the worst scenarios of loss, grief, betrayal, and life-threatening danger. But remember that I will work *all* things together for good as you partner with Me in two things: firstly, that you practice your love with Me so that fear, anger, and debilitating emotions will not put a chokehold on your heart; secondly, that you focus on the purpose that I have for you in this circumstance. Your alliance with Me must be specific and strong.

I will help you with the stance you need to adopt in your circum*stance.* If your response is vague and weak, you will become double-minded and therefore incapable of receiving. This is called process: learning the way, the truth, and the life of Jesus within. Most people want to bypass process and go straight to a successful outcome. However, it's the process that makes you rich in your identity and developed character. Not taking the opportunity to process properly guarantees that you will have to take the test again, simply because you will not have received all the good I wanted to release!

It is the true knowledge of Jesus that I need you to explore and receive. By knowledge I mean that what you are learning becomes both an encounter with Me and an experience of Jesus. What you experience becomes your upgrade and therefore your testimony, which can be used over and over again because it is a lifestyle.

In order for you to learn and become established in Our nature as your identity, you will need some amazing, powerful, and magnificent promises. This is hugely enjoyable for Me. The promises are what guarantee your continuous upgrades as you joyfully journey with Me. By these promises, you will have constant experiences of who I am for you. In this way, you become a partaker of My nature. You become My visual aid to the world.

My undivided attention and affection are designed to bring you into a huge place of favor and personal anointing. I love to give promises! I deliberately make them magnificent and precious in your life. They will align you with My majesty. These promises will make your circumstances seem smaller by comparison. They open you up to fullness and abundance.

Nothing is ever ordinary with Me. I hope you understand that and can laugh with Me in your life situations. All of Heaven is attracted to Jesus in you! In Christ you are highly attractive to Me and I will pour out on you the same love and affection that I have for the Son. Pay attention to the oneness and unity in the Godhead because you are included in Our conversations that include discussing your purpose, identity, and lifestyle.

When you face life in Me, your circumstances are never the problem. It is your *perception* of your circumstances that can be problematic. If you view life issues from your old nature, the stress and the strain will be bigger than the problem. They will debilitate you.

Viewed from My perspective, the promise will look bigger than the issue, and your enlargement will become a significant part of the process. Your current circumstances are the ideal soil for your next breakthrough in Christ. You will not have a better opportunity than now to step up into a higher place of favor and promise. The law of acceleration, favor, divine advantage, and moving in the opposite spirit are wide open to you whenever a "problem" enters your life.

Therefore, every negative is designed to reveal its heavenly opposite so that you may grow up and learn to prosper regardless of circumstances. So, for example, a situation that appears to be daunting, intimidating, and discouraging must instead become stimulating, encouraging, and cheerful! Would I ever be disheartened, threatened, or dismayed? I am in you and I am always Lord over *all* things. I can flip every situation over to the rule of Heaven.

Beloved, no circumstance can compete with the favor that I want you to enjoy in Jesus. In real terms, you are only ever being challenged by My goodness. You are not challenged by circumstances, human opposition, or the enemy. You overcome evil with goodness; therefore, goodness is a higher challenge. It lifts you up to only see, think, and speak towards the goodness of God. This means that really you are learning to live under a weight of majesty, favor, blessing, and promises—all wrapped up in the beauty, sovereignty, and power of the indwelling Christ. He is the Author and Finisher of all the incredible plans I have directed towards you.

The question for you is, what am I writing on your heart in this present situation? What is being created in you? I am the architect of your spiritual lifestyle. Therefore, you cannot afford to see problems simply as difficulties to overcome. That's merely an earthly mindset. Instead, these difficult places are the chosen spaces where you and I are upgrading our relationship!

All situations offer up variables to the God who is unchanging and consistent. My promise to you, Beloved, is that My unchanging, consistent nature will be relentless in its opposition to all of life's negative variables.

Shall we get started?

DEEPENING MY RESPONSE TO LETTER 8

"Knowing that the gift of God is available to you is key to your current life issues. It becomes the 'stance' you take in your circum*stance*."

1. When a challenge appears, what do you want your first thought to be? Write it down.

2. Describe your usual response to receiving an extravagant gift from a friend. How does this illustrate or impact how you receive from Me?

3. How is *believing* there is a gift of God present different than *knowing* it is there?

4. Which stance do you want to take: believing or knowing?

5. What needs to upgrade in your thinking to do that?

"The gift of the Holy Spirit is given so that you can know what is available to you in any situation. He will take what belongs to Jesus and will give it to you... You overcome by what you can receive from Me when you are under pressure."

1. Describe your current relationship with the Holy Spirit. Who am I to you?

2. What part of My nature would you like to encounter more of?

3. Choose a current pressure point in your life, then consider:

   a. What is possible for you to receive from Me here?

   b. Are you fearful, worried, panicked, frustrated, angry, unbelieving, or have another negative response that overwhelms you?

   c. How is this preventing you from accepting the full
      delivery of My provision?

   d. What would you like to focus on and empower instead?

   e. What am I writing on your heart in this present situation?
      What am I creating in you?

"A gift is not a discipline—it is a delight!"

1. How would you describe the characteristics of a
   spiritual discipline?

2. And what would you say are the qualities of a delightful gift?

3. What spiritual disciplines would you like to exchange for
   spiritual delights?

"Life in the Spirit is about learning to recognize what belongs to you already because Jesus lives in you.... Then you get to call it up in you when you are under pressure."

1. So, what are you recognizing of Me in you?

2. What gifts am I delighted to give you?

3. What do you want to learn to call up in yourself
   under pressure?

"Practice the lifestyle of being in Me."

Let's learn how to gain control of circumstances and then convert that to your everyday life. Think of a common challenge that has repeatedly overwhelmed you and let's begin to love the learning together.

1. Gaining control of your circumstances:

   a. What is the lesson this situation allows you to practice?

b. Write down the response you want to have.

c. How can you rehearse this during your day?

d. Keep track of your practices. How many a day do you average after a week?

e. What are you learning about making your rehearsals enjoyable?

f. Who are you excited to become?

g. What is upgrading in our relationship?

2. Establishing a lifestyle:

a. Who have I been to you that you've not experienced before?

b. Who are you becoming more of in Me?

c. In what ways does this new rhythm make our life together better?

d. What mindsets and behaviors are easier now than when you started?

e. Where else can you apply what we're learning together?

f. Describe your new normal after a few weeks.

"In every situation you face, He is the door to all your possibilities."

1. What is the door of opportunity that Jesus wants to be for you in your current situation?

2. What do you need an entrance into?

3. What do you need an exit from?

4. Describe the response you want to have when you hear Me knocking.

"We agreed that I, the Comforter, would need to live inside of you because We have always intended to take you out of your comfort zone."

1. Where am I moving you out of a comfort zone?

2. What was comfortable about it?

3. What type of comfort will I be for you here?

4. What am I teaching you and what are you willing to unlearn?

"Never downsize My majesty because then you will downgrade your trust, faith, and favor."

1. Where have you allowed My majesty to be comfortably good but not overwhelmingly magnificent?

2. Where did that lesser thinking lead you to?

3. Where would I like to lead you instead?

4. What would an upgraded perspective of My majesty in that situation look like? Describe it.

5. What am I saying yes to that you had assumed would be a no?

6. What upgrades in your thinking and identity will you need to thrive in My yes?

"We want you to agree with Our claim on you for this circumstance. That claim comes in the form of a promise, a specific favor, or the kind intention of Our will."

Look at page 137 for a list of My promises to you.

1. What old mindset or situation do you need an upgraded perspective of?

2. What upgrade from that list am I claiming for you?

3. Write your promise(s) on small pieces of paper. Put them on your mirror, in your pocket, in your wallet, on your desk, by your kitchen sink, etc. Read your promise aloud whenever you encounter it.

4. Keep a little promise journal with you and record the times I am relentlessly pursuing this promise with you. Make thank-you notes when you read or encounter your promise.

    a. Describe how My relentless goodness challenges you.

    b. What revelation is opening up to you more?

"You can count on My unchanging nature, My relentless consistency, and My pattern of predictability. That means you can include My constancy as part of your anticipation."

1. What are the implications of this truth for our relationship and your development?

2. Where are you beginning to see patterns of predictability in your life?

3. How are you seeing more of My image in you?

4. Where are you leaning into Me in trust and faith?

"Beloved, you have My undivided attention and affection. My heart is always fully fixed on Jesus. When I include you in that same wonderful space, you become a partaker of the divine nature. I want you to establish this truth as a life value and principle that will never change."

A value is a statement of what is important to you. A principle is how that value is expressed in your life.

1. What are the implications for you of having My undivided attention and affection?

2. What are the implications for Me?

3. What is the impact of this truth on our relationship?

4. How do you want your language and actions to reflect this principle?

"Would I ever be disheartened, threatened, or dismayed? I am in you and I am always Lord over *all* things. I can flip every situation over to the rule of heaven... [You] are only ever being challenged by My goodness."

Imagine Me in Heaven, running about in dismay or depressed or disheartened. Allow that image to come to life. Does it make any sense? Of course not! Yet often My people react on Earth as if this is happening in Heaven.

1. Describe how you want your initial response to any situation to reflect Me.

2. What would it look like to be challenged by My goodness?

INVITATION TO RESPOND
Claiming Your Upgrades

Write Me a letter with the top five upgrades you want to claim. What promises are you unwrapping with each? How are you challenged by My goodness? Tell me what you're enjoying and discovering about My gifts to you!

FINAL APPLICATION

Evidences of Transformation

Your stories of personal transformation are the true mile markers on your journey. Growing up into the full image of Christ is not measured by the number of books you've read, courses completed, or teachings you've heard. It is in the maturing process of:

- Perceiving God, yourself, and your circumstances as He does

- Thinking more with the mind of Christ

- Using the same language God does when He talks about us and others

- Choosing to respond to others the way He has responded to us

Our life stories are the Evidences of Transformation, confirmation that we're becoming more like who we've been beholding. They allow us to consider, "In what ways am I becoming more like Christ?"

Evidences of Transformation are not a one-time experience, but a continuing conversation with God and with friends you may be sharing this journey with.

If you continue to assess your growth using these markers, you will be constantly encouraged. You have areas of spirituality that God is developing, and you are perceiving, thinking, speaking, and acting more like Christ now than when you started this book—and that's good news.

EVIDENCE OF TRANSFORMATION IN PERCEPTION

How you are looking and perceiving in a different way?

1. I am seeing myself through a new-man lens of God's grace and kindness.

   a. My image of myself is aligning more with His image of me.

   b. My old earth-bound perspective of myself was…

   c. Now, I see myself more as…

   d. Give one real-life example of your new lens/perception about yourself:

2. I am seeing a more accurate image of God's true nature.

   a. My old-man perspective of God was…

b. Now I am perceiving Him to be...

c. Give one real-life example of your new lens/perception about God:

EVIDENCE OF TRANSFORMATION IN MINDSETS

*How you are **thinking** about what you're perceiving.*

1. I am thinking about what I am unlearning as well as what I am learning.

   a. I am unlearning...

   b. I am learning...

   c. Give a real-life encounter of unlearning and the new mindset you've gained:

2. I not only desire a new-man lifestyle, but I am thinking more with the mind of Christ.

   a. I am desiring a new-man lifestyle in...

   b. My new-man thought that empowers that is...

c. Give one real-life example of a new-man way of thinking that supports your new-man development:

EVIDENCE OF TRANSFORMATION IN LANGUAGE

How I talk about myself, God, and others.

1. I am learning the language of my new, true identity— speaking with hope and grace about who I am and am becoming in Christ.

   a. I used to speak negatively about…

   b. I have made war on my negativity by choosing to speak…

   c. Give a real-life example of making this choice:

2. I am actively agreeing with God's promises and declaring my upgrades.

   a. I had unclaimed upgrades in…

   b. I am now declaring my promises and upgrades for…

   c. Share one real-world experience of how you've done this:

EVIDENCE OF TRANSFORMATION IN ACTIONS

How my behavioral choices have changed.

1. I am choosing new-man behaviors in response to God's empowering grace. I have greater strength and confidence to receive more of His mercy, kindness, and goodness.

   a. Instead of choosing to…

   b. I am instead choosing to…

   c. Give one real-life example of choosing to respond to God's empowering grace:

2. I am responding to my identity in Christ rather than only pursuing behavioral changes.

   a. I have discovered my identity in Christ as…

   b. I am behaving accordingly by…

   c. Share a real-life situation where you did this:

FINAL ACTIVATION

The New You

When you began reading this divine letter, you had a certain perception of yourself. As a culminating activation, let's explore what you see now.

- Review the questions you've responded to and the letters you've written back to God.

- Consider your Evidences of Transformation.

- Key question: How would you describe yourself now, using God's language about you?

As you write out your new character description, consider the following truths:

- Use your new lens. See yourself as God does, elevated into His strength and power. Resist the old habit of viewing your life through any weaknesses or perceived lack.

- Practice what you're learning about your newness advantage as well as what you are unlearning about your old perceptions of yourself.

- Think in terms of who you are and are becoming. This mindset acknowledges that you may not have arrived yet, but you're not where you used to be either!

- If there is a lack of freedom in your thinking about yourself, discover the lie that is binding you.

  - What do you believe about who you are that God doesn't?

  - What does He believe? Write about that instead!

- Read your description aloud to the Lord. It may feel awkward at first, but let His goodness, grace, and kindness encourage you. Seeing yourself as He does is a huge part of your newness advantage.

Revisit this activation every few months. Upgrade your description as you see more through His eyes. Keep each version you write. It's an additional record of transformation.

If you're sharing this book experience with friends, be daring and share your descriptions. They may see some wonderful things that you have missed!

HOW TO MAKE IT YOURS

How to take the word I promise and make it yours in the Spirit:

1. Focus on an aspect of My nature that you need at this moment (any fruit of the Spirit, grace, mercy, etc.). Rejoice that this is My gift to you right now.

2. Take several deep calming breaths from your diaphragm. Hold your breath each time at the top end and let it out slowly, as you rejoice in My Presence in you. Continue until peace and calm have dispersed any negative thought or emotion.

3. Think of your circumstance and imagine Me in it with you. Do not rush. You are practicing My Presence.

4. When you are ready, ask Me what I am seeing. Ask for wisdom and revelation to open your eyes.

5. Write down any key words, phrases, or ideas.

6. When you have a sense of what the circumstance is about, put these thoughts in the form of several keys. Keys are important because they lock up any negativity in you and bind the efforts of the opposition. They also open you up to divine purpose.

7. When you know My purpose, rejoice again, giving thanks. Let My joy be in you. Give thanks out loud and thanksgiving will create exaltation in you.

8. Ask Me for a promise or Scripture. This will be a confirmation of My intent towards you. Ask Me for an upgrade in this particular situation.

9. When you have it, study it! What is being promised?

10. Write the promise/upgrade into a declaration. (E.g., "I declare that this promise of this... (upgrade) is mine and will be fulfilled in Jesus' name.")

11. Speak it out loud with passion and faith as many times as you need/want until (a) you change and (b) the situation is resolved.

12. Keep a journal of your Scriptures, promises, thoughts, keys, and upgrades. These are gifts you can use over and over again.

SCRIPTURAL UPGRADES

Here are some scriptural upgrades to get you started in the process of learning all that I want to give you.

- **Alive unto God:** Romans 6:11; 1 Corinthians 15:22

- **All Grace Abounds Toward Us:** 2 Corinthians 9:8

- **All Sufficiency in Us Through Him:** 2 Corinthians 9:8

- **All Things Belong to Us, Including Life and Death:** 1 Corinthians 3:21-23

- **Ambassadors:** 2 Corinthians 5:20-21

- **Anointed:** 1 John 2:20, 27; Psalm 20:6

- **Apple of God's Eye:** Zechariah 2:8; Psalm 17:8

- **As He Is, So Are We on This Earth:** 1 John 2:6, 4:17

- **Baptized into Christ and into His Death:** Romans 6:3

- **Being Perfected:** Hebrews 10:14

- **Beloved:** 1 John 4:1, 7; Psalm 127:2; Colossians 3:12

- **Blameless:** 2 Peter 3:14

- **Blessed:** Romans 4:17; John 20:29

- **Blessed with All Spiritual Blessings:** Ephesians 1:3

- **Bold Access to the Throne of God:** Ephesians 2:18, 3:12; Hebrews 4:16

- **Bride:** Revelation 19:7; Isaiah 61:10-11

- **Buried with Christ in His Death:** Romans 6:4

- **Called into Fellowship with Christ:** 1 Corinthians 1:9

- **Called with a Holy Calling:** 2 Timothy 1:9

- **Can Do All Things Through Christ:** Philippians 4:13; John 15:5

- **Chosen:** John 15:16; Ephesians 1:4; 2 Thessalonians 2:13

- **Christ Indwells Us with All Fullness:** Ephesians 1:23; Colossians 2:9; John 1:16

- **Co-heirs with Christ (see "Joint"):** Romans 8:17

- **Created for Good Works:** Ephesians 2:10

- **Curse-free:** Galatians 3:13

- **Dead to Sin:** Galatians 2:20; Romans 6:2, 11

- **Dead with Christ:** Romans 6:8

- **Declared Holy:** 1 Corinthians 3:17; Colossians 3:12

- **Elect:** Romans 8:23; Colossians 3:12

- **Enriched in All Knowledge:** 1 Corinthians 1:5

- **Enriched in All Speech:** 1 Corinthians 1:5

- **Enriched, Filled:** 1 Corinthians 1:5, 4:7-8

- **Fellow Citizens of God's Household:** Ephesians 2:19

- **Free:** Galatians 3:13; John 8:32-36

- **Freed from Sin:** Romans 6:7

- **Freely Given All Things:** Romans 8:32

- **Fruitful:** Colossians 1:10

- **Gifted:** 1 Corinthians 12:1-12

- **Given All Things:** 2 Peter 1:3-4

- **Habitation of God:** Ephesians 2:22

- **Have the Mind of Christ:** 1 Corinthians 2:16; Philippians 2:5

- **He Has Been Made Rich Because of Us:** Ephesians 1:18

- **He Is at Work Within Us:** Philippians 2:13

- **He Is for Us and Not Against Us:** Romans 8:31

- **Healed:** 1 Peter 2:24

- **Hidden in Christ:** Colossians 3:13

- **Highly Favored:** Proverbs 8:35, 12:2

- **His Body:** Romans 12:1-2, 5; 1 Corinthians 6:19-20

- **His Fullness:** Ephesians 1:23; John 1:16

- **His Possession, Bought with a Price, Not Our Own:** 1 Corinthians 6:20, 7:23

- **His Workmanship:** Ephesians 2:10; Philippians 2:13; 1 Corinthians 3:9

- **Holy Priesthood:** 1 Peter 2:5

- **Increasing in the Knowledge of God:** Colossians 1:10

- **Inseparable from the Love of God in Christ:** Romans 8:38-39

- **Joint Heirs with Him:** Galatians 3:29, 4:7; Titus 3:7

- **Justified:** Romans 8:30

- **Kingdom of God Within Us:** Luke 17:20-21

- **Kings, Priests and Rulers:** Revelation 1:6

- **Known by Him:** 2 Timothy 2:19

- **Lacking in Nothing:** 1 Corinthians 1:7; 1 Thessalonians 4:12

- **Light of the World as He Is:** John 8:12; Matthew 5:14; Ephesians 5:8

- **Live by Faith:** Galatians 2:20

- **Live by God's Word:** Matthew 4:4

- **Living Stones:** 1 Peter 2:5

- **Made in His Image:** Genesis 1:26-27; Hebrews 2:7

- **Made Rich in All Things:** 2 Timothy 2:21

- **More Than Conquerors:** Romans 8:37

- **New Creation:** Galatians 6:15; 2 Corinthians 26:5

- **Of a Sound Mind:** 2 Timothy 2:7

- **Ordained:** John 15:16; Psalm 8:2

- **People of God:** 1 Peter 1:10; Psalm 100:3

- **People for His Possession:** 1 Peter 2:9; Malachi 3:17

- **Pillars of the Truth of God:** 1 Timothy 3:15

- **Prepared Unto Good Works:** 2 Timothy 2:21;
  2 Corinthians 9:8

- **Protected:** Psalm 121:18; Deuteronomy 28:6

- **Purified:** 1 Peter 1:22

- **Raised with Christ in His Resurrection Unto Life:**
  Romans 6:4

- **Redeemed:** Galatians 3:13; Revelation 5:9; 1 Peter 1:18

- **Righteousness of God in Christ Jesus:** 2 Corinthians 3:9;
  Philippians 3:9

- **Royal Priesthood:** 1 Peter 2:9

- **Saints:** Colossians 1:2; 1 Corinthians 1:2

- **Salt of the Earth:** Matthew 5:13

- **Sanctified:** 2 Timothy 2:21; Romans 15:16

- **Saved:** Ephesians 2:5; 2 Timothy 1:9

- **Sealed:** Ephesians 4:30; 2 Corinthians 1:22

- **Seated with Him in Heavenly Places:** Ephesians 1:20-21

- **Servants:** John 15:15; 1 Peter 2:16; Ephesians 6:6

- **Share His Authority:** Luke 9:1

- **Sheep of His Pasture:** John 10:7; 1 Peter 2:25; Romans 8:36

- **Sons of God:** 1 John 3:1-2; Philippians 2:15

- **Sons of Light:** John 12:36

- **Stewards/Administrators:** Luke 12:42

- **Strengthened:** Colossians 1:10-11

- **Temple of God:** 1 Corinthians 3:16-17, 6:16

- **Temple of the Holy Spirit:** 1 Corinthians 6:19

- **The Elect of God:** Colossians 3:12

- **The Friends of God:** John 15:12-17

- **The Fullness of Life and Godliness Are Ours:** 2 Peter 1:3

- **Transformed:** Romans 12:2; 2 Corinthians 11:15

- **Vessels of Glory and Honor:** Romans 9:21; 2 Timothy 2:21

- **Walk by Faith:** 2 Corinthians 5:17

- **Walk in Newness of Life, Dead to Sin:** Romans 6:2, 4

- **Warriors:** 2 Timothy 2:3

- **We Are "of" God:** 1 John 4:4

- **Wise:** 1 Corinthians 4:10

- **Witnesses:** Luke 24:48; Acts 1:18

- **Worthy of the Lord:** Colossians 1:10

ABOUT THE AUTHOR

Graham and Theresa Cooke reside in Santa Barbara, California. Working together with their closest friends, they have formed a Kingdom community of creatives and entrepreneurs. While individual members of the community are involved in a wide range of Kingdom activities (e.g., caring for the poor, teaching/ training, mentoring, and equipping), the community, as a whole, is focused on impacting the social pillars of Arts and Business in Santa Barbara. They are committed to making a place for Kingdom-minded dreamers to explore and realize the potential of their imagination—and to raising the "water level" of Kingdom culture in this city.

Graham is married to Theresa, who has a passion for worship and dance. She loves to be involved in intercession, mentoring, and setting people free. She cares about injustice, abuse and has compassion for people who are sick, suffering, and disenfranchised. They have a growing family spanning two generations and several countries. All their children are involved in some aspect of creativity, leadership, business, the arts, and entertainment. There are numerous grandchildren who keep them busy laughing and enjoying life.

Well known as a popular conference speaker, Graham also offers training programs on the prophetic, spiritual warfare, intimacy and devotional life, leadership, spirituality, and the church in transition. He particularly loves to explore the new man in Jesus and is passionate about people discovering their true selves in Christ. He functions as a consultant and free-thinker to businesses, churches, and organizations, enabling them to develop strategically. He has a passion to establish the Kingdom and build prototype communities that can fully reach a post-modern society.

A strong part of Graham's ministry is in producing finances and resources for the poor and disenfranchised in developing countries. He supports many projects specifically for widows, orphans, and people in the penal system. He hates the abuse of women and works actively against human trafficking and the sex slave trade—including women caught up in prostitution and pornography.

Graham is an ambassador to communities of faith in the Body of Christ on behalf of Not For Sale. He talks about the work of Not For Sale and empowers individuals, families, businesses, ministries, and churches to get involved in sponsoring projects. Not For Sale has specific assignments that involve rescue, restoration, providing education, skills-based training, and small business development to enable people to become fully rehabilitated into a normal, productive life.

If you would like to invite Graham to minister at an event, please complete our online Ministry Invitation Form at: *www.BrilliantPerspectives.com*

If you want to give to Not For Sale and partner with them directly, it's simple. Go to their website: *www.NotForSaleCampaign.org*

Look at the range of what they are doing and at the very least give a one-time gift, or give a monthly donation for six months or one year. Better still, involve your family, friends, business, or church in sponsoring a specific project. Your contribution makes a world of difference to the people rescued because of your involvement.

BOOK 3

BUILDING THE RIGHT MINDSET

The Letters from God Series

———

Every action is rooted in the thought that produced it.

Right thinking will always generate faith.

Renewing the mind and transformation are inseparable.

The mind of Christ is full of possibilities.

A person in two minds will never be effective.

Relational thinking is the key to experiencing Sonship.

Alignment is critical to overcoming

Spiritual appraisal gives us access to hidden wisdom.

Learn how to combine spiritual thoughts
with spiritual words in a way that opens up the
Kingdom with insight and power.

———

COMING SOON!
www.BrilliantBookHouse.com

Join Graham Cooke & friends @

BrilliantPerspectives.com

- ✓ *Weekly Perspective*
- ✓ *Dynamic Conversation*
- ✓ *Free Products*
- ✓ *Q&A's w Graham*
- ✓ *And More...*

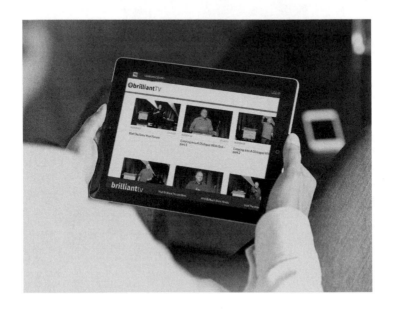

brilliantTV.com

Be part of an online mentoring class
and access a growing video library
of teachings by Graham Cooke for
one low monthly subscription.

optimized for mobile devices
available anywhere with internet or network connection

NOT FOR SALE 💲

GOODNESS IN ACTION, POWERFULLY!

NOT FOR SALE protects people and communities around the world from modern-day slavery and human trafficking Through business, education, job training, providing homes, long-term care, health & rescue, legal support, and rehabilitation.

BRILLIANT is honored to act as an Ambassador for this great organization, by raising funds and awareness.

END SLAVERY NOW!
YOUR HELP MATTERS

www.notforsalecampaign.org